# String Quilts

## 10 Fun Patterns for Innovating and Renovating

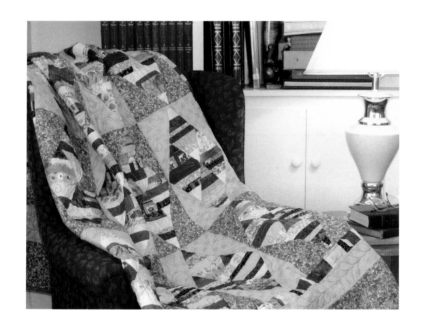

### A SCRAP QUILT BOOK
by *Elsie M. Campbell*

**Good Books**

Intercourse, PA  17534
800/762-7171
www.GoodBooks.com

Photo credits: front and back cover, title page, pages 36, 58
by Stephanie Willoughby Stewart; pages 7, 9–11, 14 by
Elsie Campbell; all other photos by Kenneth Campbell.

Illustrations and diagrams by Cynthia Vierthaler

Design by Cliff Snyder

**STRING QUILTS**

Copyright © 2009 by Good Books, Intercourse, PA 17534

International Standard Book Number: 978-1-56148-675-5
Library of Congress Catalog Card Number: 2009019706

**Library of Congress Cataloging-in-Publication Data**
Campbell, Elsie, 1949-
  String quilts : a scrap quilt book / by Elsie M. Campbell.
    p. cm.
  ISBN 978-1-56148-675-5 (pbk. : alk. paper) 1. Patchwork--Patterns.
2. Quilting--Patterns. I. Title.
  TT835.C3566 2009
  746.46′041--dc22                                      2009019706

# Table of Contents

4    Introduction

6    Elsie's Top Tips for Successful String Quilts

21   Purple Pride

25   Purple Posies

31   Unique Batik

35   Pots of Flowers

41   Dad's Plaids

47   Plaid Poppies

53   Picket Fence

57   Diamond in the Rough

63   Autumn Stars

69   Square Dance

72   Gallery of String Quilts

79   Resources

80   Acknowledgments

80   About the Author

# Introduction

My earliest memories include string quilts. Shortly after I was born, my maternal grandmother lovingly stitched a string quilt for my crib from bits and pieces of old clothing and scraps left over from her hand-made dresses. For the foundations, she cut squares from still-usable parts of worn household linens like bed sheets and dish towels. The strips and pieces from the clothing were stitched to the foundation squares, and then those squares were sewn together to make the quilt top.

Grandma didn't even buy new batting for her quilts. She simply cut the least worn parts from an old cotton flannel blanket and used that as the middle part of the quilt. Another piece of flannel for the backing, and a few yarn ties, and my crib quilt was complete. This quilt became my "blankie," my comfort when things didn't go as I wished. My sister and I used this little quilt as the "door" when we made tents over the clothesline. Sometimes we hid under our quilts to read a book by flashlight so Mom wouldn't know when we stayed up past our bedtimes. I still love this quilt for all the memories attached to it; I wouldn't trade it for any other quilt in the world.

Even though I now make much larger and more complicated quilts with elaborate patterns, I still love to make string quilts for my grown children and other family members—to use as throws on a bed or couch, to stay warm at outdoor events, or to cover the ground for picnics. When I make string quilts, I don't usually plan every piece before cutting and sewing strips together. I just begin stitching scrap pieces of fabric together, enjoying the process with the knowledge that I am making something useful.

Making string quilts is a playful process, but making "sister string quilts," even more so. I have two sisters; we are close in age and have shared many of the same interests and activities while growing up. Linda teaches piano at the college level; Helen loves to knit, both by hand and machine, and has designed and published patterns for knitting. Of course you already know

that my passion is quiltmaking. Even though my sisters and I have different looks and interests, my mother would say, "But you are cut from the same cloth!"

The sister quilts that are patterned in this book resulted from my experimenting with scraps left over from the Purple Pride string-pieced quilt (see page 21). I wanted to make a medallion quilt, spontaneous in nature. I drew flower shapes on the paper side of paper-backed fusible webbing, and then fused that to the wrong side of the scraps and cut them out. I stitched a background and started placing the flower shapes on the background. I added leaves and stems. Then I decided to add

*This crib quilt was lovingly made by my maternal grandmother, Katherine Fast Goebel, from scraps of used clothing, most notably one of the shirts worn by her husband, John William Goebel. My grandmother used a piece of a used cotton blanket as the batting. She never threw away anything that could be incorporated into a quilt.*

a bow to hold the stems together. The resulting arrangement was so happy and free! The process for making this quilt was like nothing I'd ever attempted before. I thoroughly enjoyed the freedom of not planning every piece before I started. Purple Posies is a charming quilt, whether used on a bed or hung on a wall.

Since then, I have made lots of sister string quilts, in addition to the six in this book. You can do it, too. Make a pieced quilt and save the scraps for the appliqué sister. Or start with strings for the appliqué quilt. You don't have to ever get around to making the pieced sister if you don't want to.

Finally, I include a Gallery of 17 string-pieced quilts made by other quilters. These showcase the range of styles that is possible with string quilts.

Of all the quilts I make, I probably feel most sentimental about my string quilts because of the fond memories I associate with their use. These are the quilts I make to be loved, used, and enjoyed. They probably won't survive 200 years into the future, but that is not why I make them. I make them to use up otherwise unusable bits of fabric left over from more intricate projects. I make them for the intense creativity and pleasure I feel from working spontaneously. I make them because I want to

make them. This is my playtime, my occasional break from making precision pieced and appliquéd beauties.

My grandmother made quilts because she needed to keep her family warm in winter. What she did out of necessity and from scarcity of materials, I now do for my own pleasure and from an abundance of fabrics.

For whatever reason you love to make quilts, I hope you find something in this book to inspire you. Whether you choose to make a quilt exactly like those patterned in this volume, or simply glean ideas for adapting patterns with your own personal touch, my purpose for this book is to help you have fun making string quilts.

May you enjoy the creative process!

*The author, Elsie (left), with her sisters, Linda (center) and Helen (right).*

# Elsie's Top Tips for Successful String Quilts

## Choose colors that you like

One of the first questions that most quilters ask themselves when planning a quilt is, " What colors should I use to make my quilt?" It can become confusing with so many beautiful fabrics and colors to choose from in today's quilt shops.

Color is an integral part of our lives from the very beginning. If you wish to start a conversation with a preschooler, one of the first questions you may ask is, "What is your favorite color?" He or she will probably respond quickly. She knows which color is her favorite without having to stop and think about it too much. Can you name your favorite color? Most likely it's on the tip of your tongue. Now, can you tell me *why* it's your favorite color? This answer probably requires a little more thought.

As adults, we tend to wear colors that make us look and feel our best. The colors we choose to wear may reflect our mood or our outlook on any particular day. When I teach my string-piecing class, the supply list includes strips and scraps of fabrics. Class participants spend the morning stitching their "strings" together to make "string-pieced yardage." When each person has sewn a panel of about a yard or so in length, I instruct them to press the seams flat in one direction, and then cut blocks or pieces for blocks from the pieced-and-pressed panel.

Then the real fun begins! Each participant plays with her blocks on a design wall until she finds a pleasing arrangement. Sometimes wonderful surprises happen. It's always amazing to see the variety of ideas that emerge from this design play. I love to take photographs of the designs in progress, and often I try to include the artist in the photograph.

After taking photos in several classes, I realized that the colors and styles of participants' clothing were subtly reflected in the colors, blocks, and patterns that emerged on the design wall! It became clear to me that each quilter chose to work with fabrics in colors that she was most comfortable wearing. Does this hypothesis hold true for you, too? Check out the colors hanging in your closet, and then examine your fabric stash. How do they compare? If you want to learn more about color and color theory, refer to some of my favorite books in the Resources list on page 79.

## Value is more important than color

Even though the colors may be what draw you to a particular quilt, it is actually *contrast in value* that creates the pattern. In other words, *value is more important than color* when making quilts. This is especially important for scrap quilts where lots of different prints and colors are combined in one project.

Why is value more important than color? I believe it's because your eye perceives light and dark (value) before it perceives color. Research has shown that a newborn's eyes perceive light and dark first; color perception develops later. When viewing something from a distance or in dim light, the first thing you notice is the object's shape, especially if it's in high contrast with the background. You can tell what kind of tree you see on the horizon simply by the shape. You don't have to know if it's green or brown or any other color to know that it's a tree.

When viewing quilts displayed at a show, the quilts I notice first are those that have striking designs in highly contrasting fabrics. They beckon me to come closer. As I draw closer, I can then identify the block pattern and individual colors. When I move in very close to the quilt, I love to examine the detail and workmanship. Each of these elements is important in determining which quilt wins the award, but the first impression is always created by contrast and value. That is not to say that soft contrast cannot be successful, but it takes more skill to achieve success with low contrast.

*Choose a wide range of values for your quilt, such as lights, mediums, and darks, as shown here. For colors, you may carefully control the range of color, choosing a traditional color scheme such as complementary, analogous, monochromatic, and so on. Or you can include every color of the rainbow. Whatever your color choice, a wide range of values is critical.*

# Sew before you cut

My grandmother pieced string quilts on cloth foundations using squares cut from recycled clothing, worn dishtowels, or old sheets. You certainly can make string quilts using foundations of fabric or paper. The foundation fabric is left in the finished quilt and paper must be removed. I prefer not to have that second layer of fabric creating bulk in my quilts, and I certainly don't like the time-consuming task of removing paper foundations.

When I make string quilts, I simply sew together strips of leftover fabrics along their length until I have a pieced panel that is a yard or more in length. Then I press all the seams in one direction, stabilizing the panel with a heavy starch mixture as I press, and then I cut blocks or appliqué pieces from the pieced panel.

To make string-pieced yardage, start with strips of fabric that range from 1" to 3" in width. The strings can be any length, but mine are usually 22" (the length of a Fat Quarter, which are 18" × 22" pieces sold in fabric shops) or 44" in length, the entire width of fabric as it is cut from the bolt. Shorter lengths can be sewn together to make longer strips, if needed.

The strings can be actual scraps from other quilts, sewing projects, and usable parts of recycled clothing, or they can be cut from new yardage or Fat Quarters of fabric. I collect most of my strings by purposefully cutting 1" to 3" strips from the uneven ends of fabric when I'm squaring up the yardage for other projects.

Sort the strings by value into piles. I usually sort my scraps into three piles by value: lights, mediums, and darks. Fabric strips also may be sorted by color for specific planned projects. One of my friends likes to sort her strings into paper bags and pull blindly from the bags when sewing strips together. She feels she gets a more random look and isn't as tempted to over-think the process.

I usually just make piles on the sewing table or on the floor around me. Sometimes I start stitching the strips together with a plan in mind, but most times I don't know where my project is headed until I have some strips sewn together.

*This is me at my sewing table getting ready to start sewing strips together for Unique Batik. I sorted my strips by both color and value before sewing them together. I didn't know at that time what shape or size blocks I was going to cut from the resulting pieced yardage. I simply wanted to have fun sewing these beautiful batik strings together and see what emerged from the process.*

## Tip #4

# Throw out the rules
## (But only for string-piecing the new yardage!)

For the next step, forget all those rules you've learned in previous quilting classes. Just sew with abandon, and relax and enjoy the creative process!

**You have my permission to break the perfect scant ¼" seam rule.** It's not important at this stage to stitch with an exact ¼" seam, as long as you have *at least* a ¼" seam. Any less than a ¼" seam and your quilt may develop holes later. Chain-piece when possible, and continue adding strings to the panel until it measures a yard or more in length. When cutting the blocks from your pieced panel, you can always add more strips to it later, if

needed, so don't be too concerned about the length of your panel.

The quilt patterns included in this book specify the length and number of panels you need for making that quilt. If there is an order for colors and/or values needed for the string-pieced panel, the directions will give you guidelines, but understand that you always have the freedom to adapt the guidelines to your own ideas.

*Note: Because children usually have an innate freedom and sense of color but sometimes lack the eye-hand coordination to stitch exact seams, making string-pieced yardage is a great activity to share with them.*

**You have my permission to have uneven, bumpy, or curved seams.** It doesn't matter at this point if the panel sides are uneven, or if the panel has a few small ripples or bumps in it. After cutting the smaller pieces or blocks from this panel, the ripples and bumps, "smiles" and "rainbows" will disappear. Don't worry about the ends of strips coming out evenly, either. Those ends will not be a part of your finished quilt.

**You have my permission to play with color and value.** There are no wrong color choices when making string quilts. In my opinion, the more, the merrier. However, if you have a planned pattern, pay attention to value placement.

**You have my permission *not* to match all your seams.** Sometimes unusual or unmatched seams are more interesting than perfect repetition of pattern. Unexpected twists in patterns and designs work together to hold the viewer's attention a little longer. Do you like puzzles? If a pattern is not complete, or if parts are missing or turned differently, your brain tends to complete the picture. It's simply more fun to figure out what elements keep you coming back to the quilt.

**You have my permission *not* to press seams as you go.** As a matter of fact, every time fabric is pressed, there's more chance for distortion. Pressing is important, but it's not necessary each time you stitch a seam. Do stop to press before your panel is too large to manage easily at the ironing board; simply slide your iron over the panel. (Remember that the rules all apply after you've cut your blocks and as you piece the blocks together.)

Press all the panel seams in one direction. There should be no pleats or creases on the front side of the panel. I like to press from the wrong side first, holding the opposite end with my free hand, and ironing in the direction I want the seams to go. I tug slightly with my free hand to assure that pleats are not developing on the front as I press.

Turn the panel over to the right side and spritz with starch or fabric sizing. I like to use a liquid starch mixed one-to-one with water in a plant-mister bottle. It's economical and doesn't have any noticeable fragrance. By making my own

*I like to press all the seams of a pieced panel in one direction. Starting on the wrong side, I hold the left portion of the panel with my left hand (as a right-handed person) and run the iron from right to left, pressing the seams to one side. Use a dry iron for this step at a setting appropriate for the fabrics used in the panel.*

**Note:** *Protect your ironing surface before using starch or fusibles. For small projects, try adhering a piece of freezer paper to the ironing board before you start. When it's soiled, remove and discard. For larger projects, cover the ironing surface with an old terry cloth beach towel. Remove it and put it through the laundry when it becomes soiled.*

starch mixture, I have control over how heavy the starched finish becomes.

After applying the starch mixture, it's important to press, *not* slide, the iron, because fabric distorts easily while damp. Press the panel until it's completely dry; this may take some time. It's normal for the iron to stick a little and for flaking on darker fabrics to occur. This flaking usually disappears as you work with the fabric and will wash out when the quilt is laundered later. Be sure to keep your iron clean, either with a commercial hot iron cleaner or with a damp cloth when cool.

TIP #5

# Cut the blocks or appliqués from the string-pieced yardage

**Use rulers.** Pick a shape, any shape, and cut your pieces. I like to choose one of my many rotary-cutting rulers and cut blocks that shape. This may be a square (6", 8", or 9½") or maybe a triangle (45° or 60°) or even a diamond—whatever strikes me at the moment.

**Use freezer-paper templates.** If the quilt has curved or odd-shaped pieces in the block, I like to use freezer-paper templates. Freezer paper is a product that's designed to keep food fresh in the freezer. It has a plastic vapor barrier on one side and paper on the other. The plastic layer will

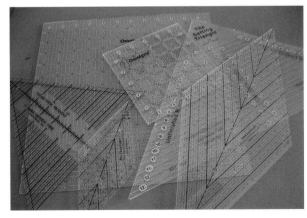

*When cutting blocks, keep it simple. Use rulers in shapes and sizes that you already own.*

*Note: When cutting your blocks, remember to keep your new seam line at least ¼" away from the seams in the string-pieced panels. You don't want to deal with two seams that fall in nearly the same line.*

adhere to fabric when pressed from the paper side with a hot, dry iron, and it's easy to remove when you're finished.

Trace the pattern shape with or without seam allowances onto the paper side of the freezer paper and cut out the shape. I prefer to use the template without seam allowances because it's easy to accidentally trim away a little of the freezer-paper template each time I cut out a piece. Over time this may change the size and shape of the template.

After making the template, adhere it to the right side of the string-pieced panel. The placement may be carefully planned or not. You may choose to let the pieces fall where they may!

Use a rotary cutter and ruler to cut straight lines by placing the edge of the ruler along the edge of the template. If you've made templates without the seam allowance, lay the ¼" line of the ruler along the edge of the template.

Use a sharp scissors to cut curves. Be sure to add the ¼" seam allowance if you've not added it

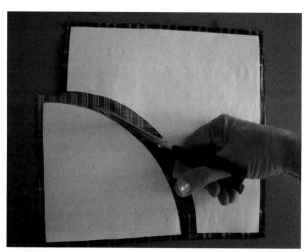

*When using freezer-paper templates for cutting blocks, cut straight lines with the rotary cutter and a ruler. Cut curved edges with a sharp scissors. If using templates without seam allowances, be sure to cut ¼" away from the template edge, as shown here.*

to your template. I like to "eyeball" it, but you may mark the cutting line if you wish.

**Use paper-backed fusible web.** Paper-backed fusible web is a product used to bond fabric to fabric. Some products form a temporary bond; others are designed to create a permanent bond. Look for a product that is compatible with the fabrics you are using in your quilt, i.e., cotton. I use the Cotton setting on my iron since I prefer that the fusible remain stable, without disappearing or staining the fabric. The fusible web should leave the fabric supple, and should not leave a residue on your needle while you finish the edges, either by hand or by machine. Check out the Resources on page 79 for my favorite product.

Trace the appliqué patterns on the paper side of the fusible web. Use pencil, or better yet a permanent ink, like an ultra-fine line Sharpie™ marker or .005 Sakura Pigma Pen. Remember that these designs will be reversed in your finished piece. This is most important if you're making lettering.

Cut the marked fusible web designs out loosely, about ⅛" to ¼" outside the marked lines. Adhere the fusible pieces to the *wrong* side of the pieced panels or scraps. Then cut out the pieces exactly on the lines.

For play on the design wall, remove the paper backing. (You may need to use pins to hold the pieces in place on the wall.) Place the background fabric or pieced background panel on the design wall. Then position the appliqué pieces as you wish on the prepared background. (If you used a sticky-backed fusible product like Steam-a-Seam 2, you can proceed to the next paragraph.) When you're satisfied with your design, gently tack the appliqué pieces in place by touching them lightly on the right side with a hot iron. A small craft iron works well for this step.

Remove the background from the design wall with the appliqués tacked in place and lay the piece on the ironing board. Permanently affix the pieces by fusing them in place on the background according to the instructions for your particular fusible web.

Because the edges of these appliqués have loose gaps where there are seams, it's imperative that all the raw edges be finished in some manner. My favorite ways are with machine satin stitch, blanket stitch by hand or by machine, or free-motion straight machine stitching.

*After you've created an arrangement of appliqués that you like, tack them in place by touching the appliqués gently with a hot, dry iron. You may eliminate this step if you've used a sticky-backed fusible product.*

**Reproducing appliqué line drawings.** The quilt patterns in this book include a scaled line drawing of the suggested appliqué placement. I encourage you to design your own appliqué placement by playing on the design wall. However, if you prefer to use appliqué shapes and placements identical to mine, you may enlarge the line drawings and use them to create the appliqué shapes and placements.

There are several ways to enlarge the drawings. First and simplest is to take this book to your local copy shop and have the technician there help you print an enlarged copy. Some shops may even have the capability to print the pattern on a very large single sheet of paper. Others will need to print them out on a series of smaller sheets of paper that may be taped or glued together, matching pattern lines. Costs vary by copy shop and by size and number of sheets of paper.

Some shops refuse to make copies from a copyrighted book. Please be assured that you may make copies of these line drawings for the purpose of reproducing the quilt. (You may not make copies to pass on to friends or to make quilts that will be sold for profit. Please see the copyright language on the page opposite the Table of Contents about the use of these patterns.)

Another way is to use your home printer. Most now have the capability to enlarge a document, but only to about 200% of the original. If you enlarge a drawing 200% and then enlarge the enlargement another 200%, you've now enlarged the original drawing by 400%. If you want to enlarge it to 500%, simply enlarge the 400% drawing another 125%. You will probably use lots of typing paper for these copies, and it may take a little experimentation to find the exact placement on the copier to get each portion of the design for the finished product. You'll then need to take a bit of time and tape, piecing all the pages together. But this is an alternative to going to a copy shop.

A third way to reproduce the appliqué line drawings is to scan the page with your home printer/scanner and save the image to your computer. Many families now have digital projectors. I own one that I use for my presentations to large groups. If you don't own one, you may be able to borrow one from a friend or rent one from your local library, office supply store, or school. Connect the projector to your computer, project the image on a large piece of paper taped to a wall, and begin tracing. Be sure that the image is true and square by using the "keystone" adjustment. You may enlarge the image by moving either the paper or the projector farther away from each other. For a large piece of paper, join two or more pieces of freezer paper by overlapping the edges about ½" and ironing over the seam with a hot, dry iron (on the paper side, of course).

Another way is to use a simple opaque projector. These are usually sold at hobby and art supply stores. There are small, inexpensive tabletop models that do a fine job. As described above, tape a large piece of paper on a wall. Place the line drawing page on the projector's surface, and turn on the projector. The light is reflected off the drawing and enlarged and focused on the wall with the paper.

TIP #6

# Keep it simple

The more quilts I make, the more I realize that simple blocks are more versatile than blocks with lots of little pieces. (Plus, they are so much easier to sew!) This is particularly true for string-pieced quilts. Large pieces and blocks are important because the yardage from which the pieces are cut is already made up of lots of different strips of fabric. Simple shapes like squares, rectangles, triangles, diamonds, and large curved pieces yield the most design options.

For example, look at what you can do with simple shapes:

*60° Diamonds*

*Squares*

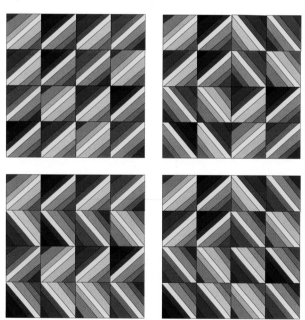

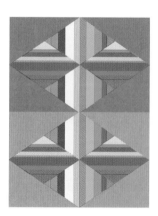

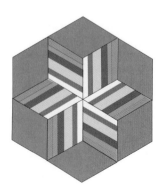

*45° Diamonds*

## TIP #7

# Play on the design wall

I used to think that a design wall was a luxury—something I didn't really need. I've changed my mind. Laying out blocks on the floor or on a bed is tough on my aging body. Plus, viewing the design vertically has more impact than when viewing it horizontally.

Design walls can be simple or complex. There are so many ideas and ways to make them. Or you can buy collapsible ones made from flannel sheets and poles that assemble like tents.

I'm an "empty nester"—that wonderful time of life when the children are grown and doing well, and I can have a room dedicated to my quilting. I made my own permanent design wall by stapling a firm, flat cotton batting to an eight-foot long wooden slat. I then rolled the slat to the underside and nailed the whole thing to the wall, just under the ceiling. Then I nailed long pieces of white

finishing trim, like those used to finish seams in paneling, around the remaining sides of the batting, stretching the batting taut and flat. With a new, sharp utility blade, I trimmed the excess batting outside the edges of the trim. My wall is permanent, flat, simple, and cheap. Yet it can be dismantled easily when we decide to build our retirement home and move. Just pull out the nails, fill the nail holes, touch up the paint, and the wall is back to normal.

When traveling and teaching, I've found that the most convenient design wall for the classroom is an inexpensive flannel-backed tablecloth taped to the wall with the flannel side out. I suggest students bring their own to class. If there isn't time in class to finish stitching the project together, the tablecloth is rolled up or carefully folded and the quilt pieces remain in place. This is also a great temporary design wall if your sewing space doubles as the dining room or living room. If guests are coming, the design wall can be put away quickly and easily without rearranging your work. When guests leave, the design wall can be pulled out to transform the space back into a sewing room.

There are so many other ideas for design walls. Do a search online to find more ideas for making one that suits your needs.

## TIP #8

# Finish that quilt

**Mitered corners.** I don't usually miter border corners unless I'm matching stripes, but well-executed mitered corners can be very attractive. Borders must be longer than the finished length to allow for mitering. The patterns that have mitered borders allow for that when giving the length measurements.

To miter corners, you must backstitch ¼" from the ends of both seams. The stitching must not overlap where the corners meet. After stitching the borders on all four sides of the quilt, lay the quilt on the ironing surface with the right side up and the border corner completely on the ironing surface. Overlap the excess borders, and fold the top border at a 45° angle over the opposing border, aligning all cut edges *(Diagram 1)*.

*Diagram 1*

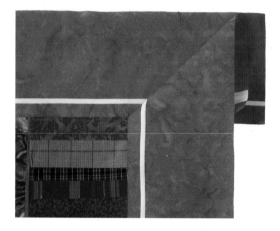

Use a large square ruler to check that the angle formed by the fold is a true 45° angle and that the outer edges of the border are square. Carefully match any stripes or multiple borders at this point. When you're satisfied with the miter, press.

Use several small strips of freezer paper as basting tape. Place the strips over the pressed miter and adhere them in place *(Diagram 2)*.

*Diagram 2*

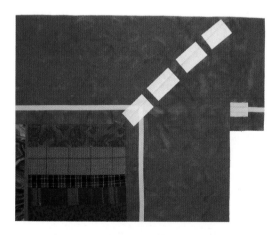

Move the quilt to the sewing machine. Working from the wrong side, open the pressed fold and stitch in the fold, stopping and backstitching ¼" from the inner edge of the miter *(Diagram 3)*.

*Diagram 3*

Open the seam and check the miter. If you're satisfied with the mitered seam, remove the freezer-paper strips from the right side and trim the seam allowances to ¼". Press the seam open *(Diagram 4)*.

*Diagram 4*

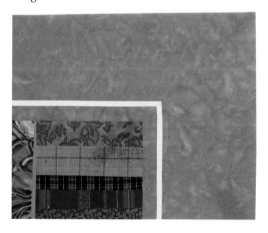

**Quilting suggestions.** Repetition creates unity in quilts. Whenever possible, I love to repeat part of the piecing and/or appliqué pattern in the quilting.

Other suggestions include straight line quilting juxtaposed with curves, or curved lines with straight. Feathers even find their way into borders around my string quilts. Study quilts at shows for ideas for quilting, or better yet, if you don't like this part of the process, let your long-arm quilter be creative with your quilt top.

String quilts tend to be very busy by their very nature because they incorporate so many different fabrics into one piece. Keep the quilting patterns simple. Most quilting stitches are not going to show up well against so many different prints anyway.

Save the fancy quilting for the plain areas. Be sure to stabilize the string-pieced areas with easy patterns or stitch-in-the-ditch quilting.

**Bias Strips / Piping.** At lease one of the quilts patterned in this book calls for piping. It takes a little extra work to make your own, but the results are worth it. To make piping, you'll need ½ yard of fabric for the piping and #3 perle cotton that has been pre-shrunk by soaking it in warm water and allowing it to air dry. For piping to have greater impact, I like to use solids for the piping, not prints. However, stripes can be very effective for piping.

On a cutting mat, fold the fabric diagonally, matching a cut edge to the adjacent selvage *(Diagram 5)*.

*Diagram 6*

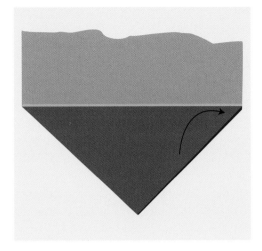

*Diagram 5*

*Diagram 7*

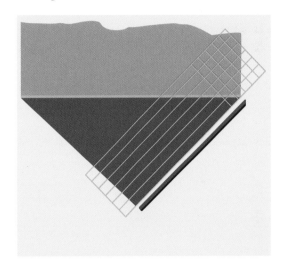

Now fold the fold back on itself to make rotary cutting easier *(Diagram 6)*. My arms are short and my shoulders are bad, so I fold it a second time because I cannot reach out much more than 18" for cutting.

Lay a rotary-cutting ruler along the fold as close to the fold as possible. Cut the fold away *(Diagram 7)*.

Bring in a second ruler and measure 1" from the cut edge. Abut the first ruler along the inside edge of the second ruler, pull the second ruler away, and make the cut, using the first ruler as the cutting edge *(Diagram 8)*.

*Diagram 8*

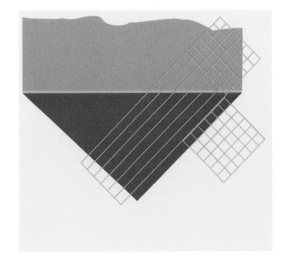

Voila! You have just cut two 1" bias strips. Continue cutting in this manner until you have the suggested number of strips for your piping.

At the sewing machine, stitch the ends of the bias strips together with diagonal seams to make one long continuous bias strip. Press these seams open.

Fold the bias strip in half lengthwise and press. There's no need to steam or to get a crisp edge. As a matter of fact, a crisp edge is *not* desirable here.

Attach a 7-groove pin-tuck foot to your sewing machine. Move the needle position so that it will stitch between the second and third grooves from the left. Wrap the perle cotton in the fold of the pressed bias *(Diagram 9)* and align it in the far left groove of the foot. Lower the foot.

*Diagram 9*

*This is a 7-groove pin-tuck foot for sewing piping; stitch between the second and third grooves from the left.*

*Note: I like to use Susan Cleveland's Piping Hot Trimming Tool for trimming the edges of the piping. See Resources on page 79 for more information.*

Stitch next to the perle cotton. You may find it helpful to run your fingernail along the bias strip to firmly "seat" the perle cotton in the fold of the bias as you stitch.

Continue stitching the entire length of the bias, being careful to keep the perle cotton encased in the fold of the bias. Trim the outer edge of the piping to exactly ¼" *(Diagram 10)*.

*Diagram 10*

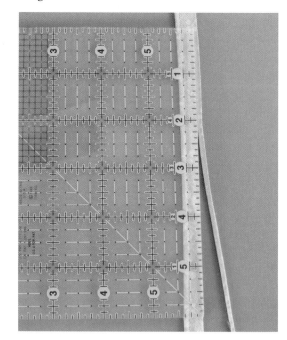

**Binding.** I prefer a straight-cut, double-fold French binding. String quilts are quite scrappy, so the binding may be scrappy, too, if you prefer.

However, some of my string quilts have borders that are cut from new yardage. When cutting these borders, I try to cut the binding at the same time as the borders. Since the fabric is already laid out on the cutting table for lengthwise strips, I simply make a few more 2"-wide cuts. This saves time, and I always know that I have enough fabric for the binding.

To prepare the quilt for binding, stay-stitch the outer edge at ¼" and trim the edges straight. For a ¼" finished binding, cut 2"-wide strips for the binding. Cut enough strips that when sewn together, end-to-end, they go entirely around the perimeter of the quilt. Sew the binding strips together with diagonal seams. Place two strips right sides together at a right angle, and stitch on the diagonal *(Diagram 11)*. Trim the seam to ¼", and press it open *(Diagram 12)*.

*Diagram 11*

*Diagram 12*

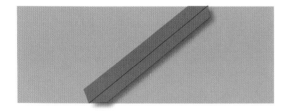

At the ironing board, press the binding strip in half lengthwise with wrong sides together. Mist the strip with a little water or starch mixture, or use a steam iron for pressing.

Lay the raw edges of the prepared binding along the trimmed edge of the front of the quilt. Begin stitching, leaving a tail of about 6" free. Use the even-feed system or a walking foot for applying the binding. Stitch ¼" from the raw edges, backstitching to start.

Stop stitching exactly ¼" from the corner with the needle down. Turn the quilt 45° and stitch to the corner of the quilt. Clip the threads and remove the quilt from the sewing machine *(Diagram 13)*.

*Diagram 13*

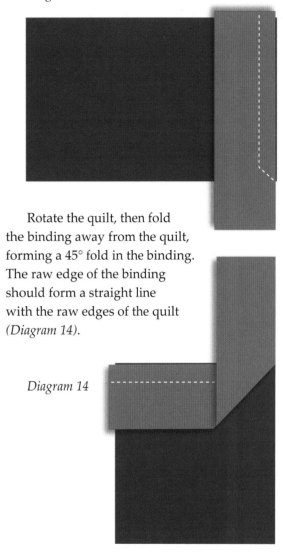

Rotate the quilt, then fold the binding away from the quilt, forming a 45° fold in the binding. The raw edge of the binding should form a straight line with the raw edges of the quilt *(Diagram 14)*.

*Diagram 14*

Fold the binding down, aligning the second fold exactly with the upper edge of the quilt. Begin

*Diagram 15*

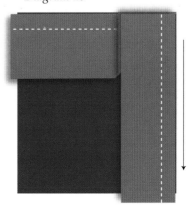

stitching at the edge of the quilt, catching the mitered pleat in the corner. When opened out, the corner should form a miter *(Diagram 15)*.

Continue stitching and turning the corners until you are about 6" from the starting point, and then backstitch. Clip the threads and remove the quilt from the machine. Lay the binding flat against the quilt, overlapping the ends. Fold the loose ends back until the folds match. Finger press a crease. Measure 1" from each crease and cut the excess binding away *(Diagram 16)*.

*Diagram 16*

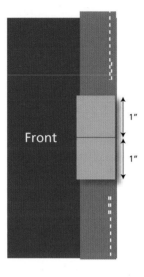

*Diagram 18*

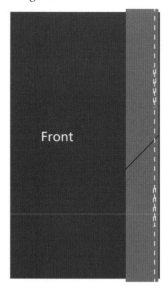

With right sides together, stitch diagonally across the trimmed ends *(Diagram 17)*. Trim the seam to ¼" and finger press the seam open. Fold the binding in half and stitch the remaining raw edges to the quilt *(Diagram 18)*.

Fold the binding to the back of the quilt and blind stitch the fold to the quilt by hand *(Diagram 19)*. Form miters at the corners and stitch the miters shut *(Diagram 20)*.

*Diagram 17*

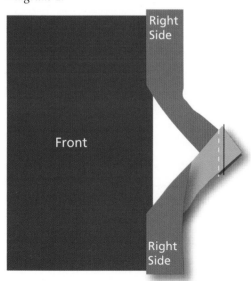

*Diagram 19*

*Diagram 20*

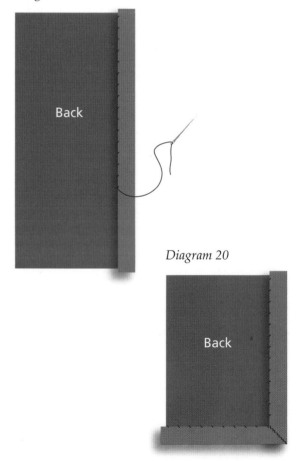

TIP #9

# Label your quilt

Take the time to label your quilt. The recipients of your quilts will be glad that you did. Include this information: The title of the quilt, your design source or inspiration, your name, the date, and where you lived when you made the quilt. If your quilt is a gift, you may want to include a little dedication or some information about the occasion for which it was made.

Use permanent ink on fabric or embroider the lettering on a separate piece of fabric. I found that ironing a piece of freezer paper to the back makes it easier to write neatly on the fabric. You can also draw straight lines on the freezer paper that will shadow through and help you write in straight lines.

Because an applied label can be removed easily or fall off with time, I think it's important also to write some of the information directly on the quilt itself. It can be hidden underneath the applied label, or be tucked in an unobvious corner, but either way historians will have this important information when your quilt becomes a museum piece.

*Sue Morgans Paul included a family tree on her label for the "Generational Quilt" (see page 76 for a photo of the quilt).*

# Purple Pride

Finished dimensions: 66" × 84"

Finished block size: 9" square

Difficulty: Beginner

## Materials

- ¼ yard each of 10 light prints, from green, teal, blue, purple, and mauve shades for a total of 2½ yards, or equivalent in scraps

- ¼ yard each of 10 medium prints, from green, teal, blue, purple, and mauve for a total of 2½ yards, or equivalent in scraps

- ¼ yard each of dark prints, from green, teal, blue, purple, and mauve for a total of 2½ yards, or equivalent in scraps

- ¼ yard each of 8 different yellow to gold prints, for the blocks and middle border, for a total of 2 yards or equivalent in scraps

- 2½ yards of dark purple print, for the inner and outer borders and binding

- 5 yards of backing fabric

- Full-size batting

Traditional string-pieced blocks get a fresh look in shades of teal, purple, and blue. Find a hidden star of bright hues lurking in the shadows of this subtle color scheme, or experiment with your own fresh setting. Nothing could be more simple to sew!

# Cutting

1 Sort the fabrics into sets of 3 by color. Include a light, medium, and dark of the same color in each set.

2 Cut various width strips across the 44" dimension from each set of prints. Strips should vary in width from approximately 2" to 3".

**Note:** *If you choose to use Fat Quarters of fabric, cut them in half across the 18" dimension to make two 9"× 22" pieces. Seam them together to make one long 9"× 44" piece before cutting the strips as described below.*

3 Cut various width strips across the 44" dimension from each of the yellow to gold prints. Strips should vary from approximately 1¾" to 2½" in width.

**Note:** *Borders are cut longer than needed to allow for trimming to exact size.*

4 Cut enough 1"-wide yellow print strips to equal 280" in length when sewn end-to-end, for the middle border.

5 Cut 2: 1½" × 75" lengthwise strips of dark purple print for the inner border.

6 Cut 2: 1½" × 60" lengthwise strips of dark purple print for the inner border.

7 Cut 2: 6" × 80" lengthwise strips of dark purple print for the outer border.

8 Cut 2: 6" × 72" lengthwise strips of dark purple print for the outer border.

9 Cut 4: 2" × 90" lengthwise strips of dark purple print for the binding.

# Directions

## STITCH THE FABRICATED YARDAGE

1 Stitch the strips together gradating through each color group in this order: light, medium, dark, *yellow*, dark, medium, light, *yellow*, light, medium, dark, *yellow*, dark, medium, light, *yellow*, etc. Make a panel in this pattern approximately 44" × 2½ yards in length. Make 4 *(Diagram 1)*.

*Diagram 1*

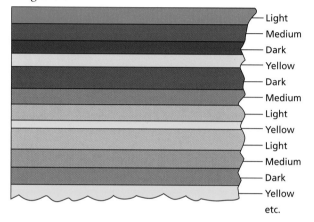

Light
Medium
Dark
Yellow
Dark
Medium
Light
Yellow
Light
Medium
Dark
Yellow
etc.

2 Press the seams in one direction, using starch to stabilize the yardage. (See page 9 in the "Top Tips" chapter for instructions on pressing and using starch).

## CUT THE BLOCKS

3 Lay the center diagonal line of a 9½" square rotary-cutting ruler on a yellow strip and cut out a block *(Diagram 2)*. Continue cutting squares in the same manner. Cut a total of 48 blocks.

*Diagram 2*

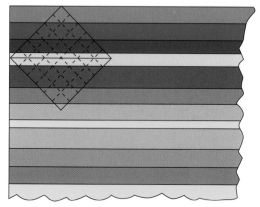

**Note:** *Freezer-paper templates may be used instead of the square ruler. Make several sets of 9½" squares of freezer paper for templates. (See page 9 in the "Top Tips" chapter for instructions on how to make and use freezer-paper templates.)*

*Vary the placement on the yellow line slightly to create movement and interest in the finished quilt.*

# Quilt Assembly

1  On the design wall, lay out your blocks in a pleasing arrangement. You may refer to the quilt photo for ideas or page 12 for other ways to set the blocks. Play around, take your time with this step, and have some fun! Your quilt doesn't need to look exactly like my version of Purple Pride. (It probably won't, so enjoy the creative process, and especially value the uniqueness of your own quilt.)

2  Stitch the blocks into rows. Press the seams of each subsequent row in opposite directions to make matching easier when joining the rows *(Diagram 3)*.

*Diagram 3*

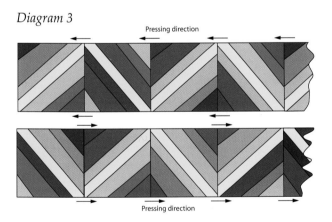

3  Join the rows, carefully matching seams. Press these seams in the same direction.

## BORDERS

4  Measure the length of the quilt. Trim the 1½" × 75" dark purple print strips to that measurement and stitch them to the sides of the quilt. Press seams toward the borders.

5  Measure the width of the quilt, including the borders. Trim the 1½" × 60" lengthwise strips of dark purple print to that measurement and stitch them to the top and bottom of the quilt. Press seams toward the borders.

6  For the middle border, stitch the remaining yellow to gold print strips end-to-end to make 4 long strips, 2 at least 80" in length and 2 at least 60" in length. Press the seams in one direction.

7  Measure the length of the quilt, including the borders. Trim the 80" strips to that measurement and sew them to the sides of the quilt.

8  In the same manner, measure the width of the quilt, cut the remaining yellow strips to that measurement, and sew them to the top and bottom of the quilt.

9  Measure, trim, and stitch the two 6" × 80" dark purple print strips to the sides of the quilt. Press the seams toward the outside of the quilt.

10  Measure, trim, and stitch the 6" × 72" dark purple print strips to the top and bottom of the quilt and press, as before.

11  Quilt as desired. Bind the quilt using the 2"-wide dark purple print strips, following the binding instructions on page 17 in the "Top Tips" chapter.

# Purple Posies

Finished dimensions: 56" × 67"
Finished block size: 5½" square
Difficulty: Intermediate

## Materials

- String-pieced scraps from Purple Pride panels (If you don't have scraps, stitch some more panels!)

- Additional ¼ yard pieces of yellow to gold prints, as needed, for the middle border

- 10 or more Fat Quarters (18" × 22") of off-white, ecru, beige, and tan prints, for the background

- ¼ yard each of 3 or 4 medium to dark prints or scraps from Purple Pride, for the binding

- 1 or 2 additional Fat Quarters of green to dark green prints or print scraps, for long stems and narrow leaves

- 4 yards of backing fabric

- Twin-size batting

- 1½ yards of paper-backed fusible web

What do you do when you have scraps left over from your string quilt? You make another string quilt, of course! I had lots of scraps left over from Purple Pride, and I hope you did, too. Those scraps give you a head start on making Purple Pride's appliqué sister, Purple Posies. Although these quilts truly are "cut from the same cloth," you know that sisters don't always look alike. So here we go…

# Cutting

### FOR THE BACKGROUND AND BORDERS

1 Cut 84: 6" squares of off-white to tan prints, for the background.

2 Cut 1"-wide bias strips from the reserved scraps of Purple Pride and stitch them together end-to-end to make a 1" -wide strip at least 160" long, for the center diamond border.

*Note: Don't bother un-stitching (ripping out) seams. Simply cut the yellow strips out with your rotary cutter. Reserve them for the middle border.*

Remove the yellow print strips from the remaining Purple Pride scraps (see Note above).

3 After the yellow strips are removed, stitch the remaining Purple Pride scraps together to make a string-pieced panel. Cut 8"-wide border strips from the pieced panel, stitching them together end-to-end, if necessary, to make two 8" × 70" borders and two 8" × 60" borders.

*Note: If necessary, cut and stitch more print strips together to make additional string-pieced yardage, according to the stitching pattern given for Purple Pride, but omitting the yellow strips.*

4 Cut enough 1"-wide assorted yellow print strips from the reserved strips to make at least 220" in length, for the middle border.

5 Cut 2"-wide strips, assorted medium to dark prints to make at least 280" in length, for the binding.

### FOR THE APPLIQUÉS

6 You may wish to enlarge the line drawing given on page 28, and trace the shapes from it, using one of the methods on page 10 in the "Top Tips" chapter. Or draw your own original flower and leaf shapes on the paper side of the paper-backed fusible web. Loosely cut out your desired number of shapes, leaving a ¼" margin outside the drawn lines.

7 Fuse the shapes to the wrong side of your pieced panels according to the manufacturer's instructions. Place flower shapes on flower colors, flower centers on yellows, and leaf shapes on green shades.

8 Cut the shapes out exactly on the drawn lines. Remove the paper backing.

9 Fuse paper-backed web to additional green to dark green print scraps or yardage. Cut long stems and narrow leaves freehand to fit and to fill in your design.

# Directions

### QUILT CENTER

1 Lay out 36 off-white to tan print 6" squares in 6 rows of 6. Stitch them into rows and join the rows to make the background center (*Diagram 1*).

*Diagram 1*

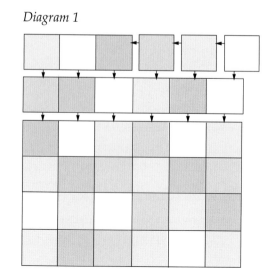

2 Cut two 33½" lengths from the 1" × 160" center diamond border strip and sew them to opposite sides of the background center.

3 In the same manner cut two 35" lengths from the remaining center diamond border strip and sew them to the remaining sides of the background center. Lay the center diamond aside.

4 In a similar manner, lay out 16 off-white to tan print 6" squares in 4 rows of 4. Stitch them into rows and join the rows to make a large square. Make 2.

5 Cut the large squares in half diagonally to make four large triangles.

6 Stitch a large triangle to each side of the center diamond *(Diagram 2)*. Note that two outer corners of the center diamond extend beyond the large triangles. Stop and backstitch ¼" from the end of the large triangles to allow the center diamond's borders to overlap the next border, leaving the corner extensions free.

*Diagram 2*

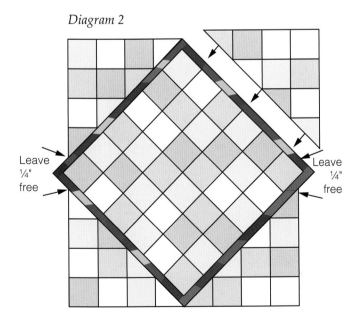

Leave ¼" free

Leave ¼" free

7 Stitch together 8 off-white to tan 6" squares to make a row. Make 2. Stitch a row to the top and bottom of the quilt.

## APPLIQUÉS

8 Place the quilt center on a design surface or wall. Remove the paper backing from the appliqué pieces and position the flower shapes as desired on the quilt center. Pin in place, if necessary. Refer to the quilt photo for placement ideas. Add stems, leaves, and ribbon shapes.

9 Lightly fuse the appliqués in place as described on page 10 in the "Top Tips" chapter. Remove any pins and place the quilt center on an ironing surface. Fuse appliqués in place, following manufacturer's instructions.

10 Finish the appliqué edges, using your choice of satin stitch, blanket stitch, or free-motion straight stitch.

## BORDERS

11 Lay out the 8"-wide pieced borders on a cutting surface. Cut them lengthwise into 1½"- and 6½"-wide inner and outer borders.

12 Stitch enough 1"-wide yellow print strips to make middle borders equal in length to the inner and outer borders. Sew the yellow middle borders between the inner and outer borders.

13 Center and stitch the 70"-long borders to the sides of the quilt, leaving the quilt center corners free. Start, stop, and backstitch ¼" from the ends.

14 Turn under the outer edges of the quilt center corners and appliqué them to the long borders.

15 Center and stitch the 60"-long borders to the top and bottom of the quilt center, starting, stopping, and backstitching ¼" from the ends.

16 Miter the corners as described on page 13 in the "Top Tips" chapter.

17 Quilt as desired. Bind the quilt using the 2"-wide lengths of assorted prints, following the binding instructions on page 17 in the "Top Tips" chapter.

**Template is at 20%**
**Enlarge on photocopier at 500%**

**Template is at 62.5%**
**Enlarge on photocopier at 160%**

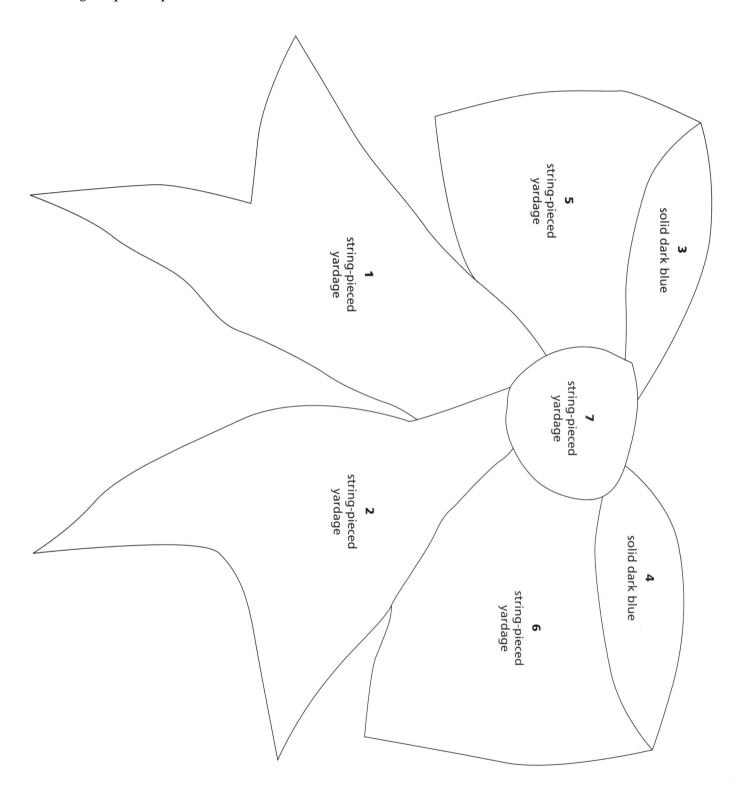

**Note:** When assembling the bow, begin with piece #1.
Stitch piece #2 onto it, assembling the bow by following
the numbers in sequence until you've used all the pieces.

# Unique Batik

Finished dimensions: 58" × 77"

Finished block size: 6¼" 60° triangles

Difficulty: Intermediate

## Materials

- 20 or more Fat Quarters of batik prints or equivalent in scraps

- 2⅔ yards of pale blue print, for the border and binding

- 5 yards of backing fabric

- Twin-sized batting

The bright, clear colors of batiks create clean, crisp lines in Unique Batik. Making this quilt was a joy. I loved grouping the fabrics by color families and stitching them together, progressing through all the hues of the rainbow. Then playing on the design wall consumed me for several days, as I tried many different arrangements of the triangles. (Yes, these diamonds started out as triangles.) Using your own creativity, you may find another way to set the blocks together, or you may choose to make one similar to mine.

# Cutting

1 Cut 1½"-wide to 3"-wide × 22"-long strips from the batiks.

*Note: Before starting, sort fabrics by value in color families (i.e., light blues, medium blues, and dark blues would be all in one color family).*

2 Cut 4: 1½" × 65" lengthwise strips of pale blue print, for the inner border.

3 Cut 4: 6½" × 75" strips of pale blue print, for the outer border.

4 Cut 9: 2" × 44" strips of pale blue print, for the binding.

# Directions

## STITCH THE FABRICATED YARDAGE

1 Sort the strips by colors and stitch them together along their length, gradating from light to dark approximately every 6" before beginning a second color family, working the pattern this time from dark to light. Make 2 panels, each approximately 3 yards in length.

*Note: Reserve 10 to 12 batik print strips for the middle border.*

2 Press seams in one direction, using starch to stabilize the panels as described on page 9 in the "Top Tips" chapter.

## CUT THE BLOCKS

3 Cut a 6"-wide strip from a panel. Lay the 60° line of a 6"-wide rotary-cutting ruler on a cut edge of the strip, and make the first cut *(Diagram 1)*.

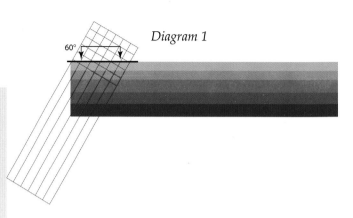

*Diagram 1*

4 Turn the ruler until the 60° line is even with the cut edge and make a second cut to make a triangle *(Diagram 2)*.

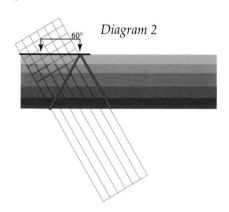

*Diagram 2*

5 Continue making cuts across the strip in the same manner. You should be able to cut 4 triangles from the strip. Two triangles will have dark points, and 2 will have light points *(Diagram 3)*. Sort the triangles into pairs with matching points. Cut a total of 69 pairs from the pieced panels.

*Diagram 3*

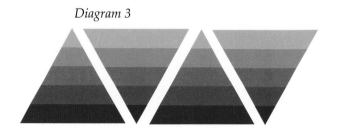

6 Stitch the paired triangles together to make 69 diamonds, at least 25 with dark centers and 44 with light centers *(Diagram 4).*

*Diagram 4*

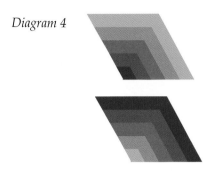

# Quilt Assembly

1 On the design wall, lay out the diamonds with dark centers in 5 rows of 5 each, to make the quilt center. Refer to the quilt photo on page 30 and Diagram 7 for placement ideas.

2 Stitch the blocks into rows and join the rows, carefully matching seams.

3 Lay out 11 diamonds with light centers in 3 rows. Stitch them into rows and join the rows, to make corner units. Make 2 corner units *(Diagram 5)* and 2 reversed corner units *(Diagram 6).* Do not trim now.

*Diagram 5*   **Corner Unit**

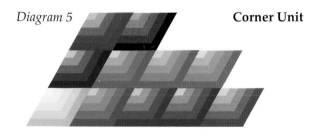

*Diagram 6*

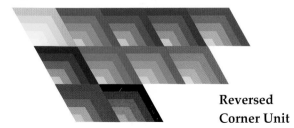

**Reversed Corner Unit**

4 Stitch the corner units to the quilt center *(Diagram 7).* Trim the outer edges straight and even.

*Diagram 7*

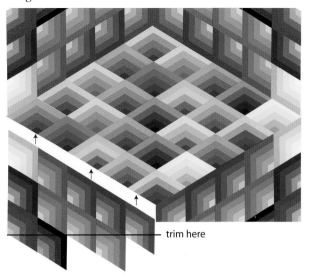

— trim here

5 Measure the length of the quilt through the center and trim two of the 1½" × 65" pale blue print strips to that measurement. Stitch them to the long sides of the quilt.

6 Measure the width of the quilt including the borders through the center of the quilt. Trim the remaining 1½" × 65" pale blue print strips to that measurement and stitch them to the short sides of the quilt.

7 Cut the reserved batik print strips into 1¼" × 11" pieces and stitch them together end-to-end to make a long middle border. This border should be approximately 200" in length.

8 Measure the length of the quilt including the borders. Cut 2 pieces of the long middle border to that length and sew them to the sides of the quilt.

9 In the same manner, measure, trim, and stitch middle borders to the top and bottom of the quilt.

10 In the same manner as for the inner borders, measure, trim, and stitch two of the 6½" × 75" pale blue print strips to the sides of the quilt.

11 Measure, trim, and stitch the remaining 6½" × 75" pale blue print strips to the top and bottom of the quilt.

12 Quilt as desired. Bind the quilt using the 2" × 44" pale blue print strips, following the binding instructions on page 17 in the "Top Tips" chapter.

# Pots of Flowers

Finished dimensions: 42" × 70"
Difficulty: Experienced (Piping, oval frame)

## Materials

- White, off-white, ecru, beige, and pastel blue print scraps or Fat Quarters (18" × 22") to equal 2 yards
- Batik print scraps in a flower color and green prints to equal 1½ yards, for the flowers and leaves
- Nine different peach, russet, and terra cotta prints at least 8" × 10", for the flower pots
- 3½ yards of blue solid, for medallion frame and binding
- ¾ yard of white solid, for the piping
- 4½ yards of backing fabric
- 4 yards of #3 perle cotton, for the piping
- Water-soluble glue stick
- Twin-size batting
- 2 yards of paper-backed fusible web (My favorite brand is Trans-Web. See Resources on page 79 for information.)

Pots of Flowers does not closely resemble its sister quilt, Unique Batik, but if you look closely, you'll see that the flowers and most of the leaves are cut from leftover strip sets from the first quilt. The flower pots are cut from new fabric, and the background is made up of rectangles of light-colored fabrics I had in my stash. Do you recognize the geranium, philodendron, larkspur, and mother-in-law's tongue? Yes, I know. Those of you who are gardeners know that I've included outdoor garden and indoor potted plants, but isn't it fun to use fabrics to create a bright and cheerful year-round garden for your home?

# Directions

### FOR THE QUILT BACKGROUND

1 Lay out the seventy-four 3½" × 5½" white, off-white, ecru, beige, and pastel blue rectangles in 9 vertical rows, offsetting them *(Diagram 1)*.

*Diagram 1*

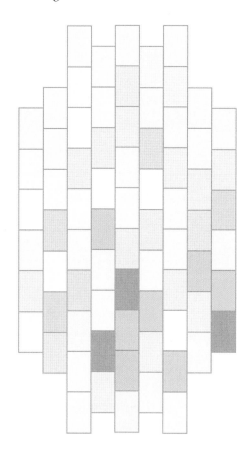

## Cutting

1 Cut 1½"-wide to 3"-wide × 22"-long strips from the batik and green prints.

2 Cut 74: 3½" × 5½" rectangles from the white, off-white, ecru, beige, and pastel blue prints, for the background.

3 Cut 1: 44" × 72" rectangle of blue solid. (You will cut the oval opening later.)

4 Cut 6: 2" × 44" strips of blue solid, for the binding.

5 Cut 3: 1" × 38" bias strips of white solid, for the piping.

2 Stitch the rectangles in vertical rows and join the rows.

### FOR THE QUILT FRAME

3 Enlarge the Pots of Flowers line drawing on page 39 by 500%. Use your enlargement to draw ¼ of the oval opening on an 18" × 36" piece of freezer paper. Mark the center. Cut ¼" inside (closer to the center) the drawn line. Use the smaller piece with the marked center as the template for your medallion frame.

4 Fold the 44" × 72" blue solid rectangle in half and in half again to divide the piece in quarters and to find the center *(Diagram 2)*.

*Diagram 2*

**Fold as marked
to find center point**

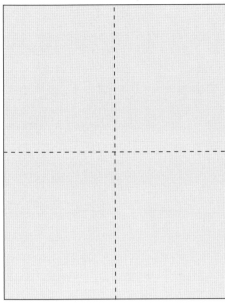

5 Adhere the freezer-paper template to one-fourth of the blue solid rectangle, matching the centers and having the straight edges of the freezer-paper template along the folds of the blue solid rectangle. Cut along the curved outline of the template. Remove the freezer-paper template and the center portion of the blue solid rectangle.

### ASSEMBLING THE BACKGROUND

6 Stitch the 1" × 38" white bias strips together end-to-end to make a long bias strip. Press the seams open, then press the long bias strip in half lengthwise.

7 Make piping using the #3 perle cotton and white bias strips, following the instructions on page 15 of the "Top Tips" chapter.

8 Stitch the piping to the cut edge of the oval openings, keeping raw edges even *(Diagram 3)*. Turn the raw edge of the piping and oval to the inside.

*Diagram 3*

raw edges

9 Position the prepared medallion frame on the background, carefully centering the background in the frame. Fold back the frame at the centers and apply glue-stick to the underside of the piping, and glue it in place on the background. Apply glue stick to the remaining portions of the frame, and glue-baste it to the background.

10 Using an edge-stitch foot, stitch the frame to the background by stitching in the ditch of the piping *(Diagram 4)*.

*Diagram 4*

## FOR THE APPLIQUÉS

11 Apply paper-backed fusible web to the wrong side of leftover green prints. Cut long narrow bias strips from the green prints and remove the paper backing. Position the strips in place on the background for stems. Fuse in place.

12 Trace the flower pot shapes from your enlarged line drawing (page 39) on the paper side of paper-backed fusible webbing. Cut the shapes out loosely and fuse them to the appropriate peach, russet, and terra cotta prints.

*Note: Each of the three flower pots is made from three different new fabrics. To achieve the 3-dimensional effect, use the darkest fabric of each set for the largest (background) shape of the rim piece and base piece. Use the medium-colored shade of fabric of each set for the second largest (foreground) shape of the rim piece and base piece, and use the lightest fabric for the accent shadowing of the rim and base pieces. Layer the background, foreground, and accent pieces in this order when applying the pot to the prepared background.*

13 Cut out the flower pot shapes. Remove the paper backing and layer them on a Teflon pressing sheet. Fuse them in place to make a flower pot. Make 3. Allow the appliqués to cool before removing from the Teflon pressing sheet.

14 Position the flower pots on the background. Refer to the quilt photo (page 34) and line drawing (page 39) for positioning.

15 To make the yardage for the flowers and leaves, stitch the batik print strips together and the green print strips together along their length to make pieced panels. I suggest stitching similar colors together. The panel for the flowers should be at least 22" × 1 yard in length, and the green prints should be about 22" × 1 yard in length, or use panel pieces left over from Unique Batik. Press the seams in one direction.

16 Use your enlarged line drawing for the flower shapes. Trace the flowers on the paper side of the fusible webbing. Loosely cut out the shapes, leaving a ¼" margin outside the drawn lines.

*Note: The geranium, larkspur, philodendron, and mother-in-law's tongue plant and flower designs are easily and effectively achieved by cutting the single but varied shapes out of the batik print strip panels. However, to maximize the design of the African violet flowers, be sure to cut each flower out individually, including the yellow centers. Layer the flowers and centers over the leaves when applying the pot to the prepared background.*

17 Fuse the shapes to the wrong side of the flower batik panel according to the manufacturer's instructions. Adhere the shapes to colors appropriate to the kind of flower depicted (for example, bright reds for the geraniums). Cut the shapes out exactly on the drawn lines. Remove the paper backing.

18 Prepare the leaf and the geranium stem shapes in a similar manner, using the green print panel for them.

19 Position the prepared flowers and leaves on the prepared quilt background, referring to your enlarged line drawing and the quilt photo for placement. Fuse the shapes in place.

20 Finish the appliqué edges, using your choice of satin stitch, blanket stitch, or free-motion straight stitch.

21 Quilt as desired. Bind the quilt using the 2" × 44" blue solid strips, following the binding instructions on page 17 in the "Top Tips" chapter.

**Template is at 20%**
**Enlarge on photocopier at 500%**

# Dad's Plaids

Finished dimensions: 72" × 90"

Finished block size: 9"

Difficulty: Intermediate

## Materials

*Note: When using recycled clothing, pay close attention to fiber content and adjust your iron temperature accordingly. Polyester and other synthetic fibers melt or scorch at the cotton setting. Avoid using shirts in which the fabric is too worn to hold up well in a quilt. Remove collars, cuffs, pockets, front plackets, and cut away the seams. Press remaining pieces flat before cutting strips from them. If you notice a lot of fading when you remove the pocket, don't use that shirt. If you don't have enough shirts, look for them at second-hand stores. You can sometimes get shirts for as little as $2 each. That's a lot of fabric for the money!*

- Approximately 25 recycled men's plaid shirts, or Fat Quarters and scraps to equal 7½ yards

- 5¼ yards of backing fabric

- ⅔ yard of a dark print or prints, for the binding

- Full- or Queen-sized batting

Dad's old plaid shirt takes on a new life as a warm and cozy quilt. If your dad doesn't want to part with his shirts, substitute plaids and stripes from your fabric stash, or do what I did and go shopping at the second-hand store. I found lots of suitable plaid shirts for very little money, and then cut off the cuffs, collars, seams, and yokes. Press the remaining portions of the shirts and cut your strips from them. Sew them together by value and color families, then cut the pieces from your pieced panels.

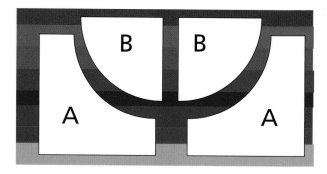

*Diagram 1*

# Cutting

1 Before beginning, sort the plaid fabrics into light and dark values. (Sort the mediums into either or both groups, as you choose.) Press them, if needed.

2 Cut 1½"-wide to 3"-wide × 22"-long strips from the plaid fabrics.

3 Cut 8: 2" × 44" strips from the dark print(s), for the binding.

# Directions

### STITCH THE FABRICATED YARDAGE

1 Stitch strips together along their length, gradually working from light to dark or from dark to light approximately every 10". Begin working a second color into the pattern only at the lightest or darkest part of the pattern. Make 3 panels, each approximately 3 yards in length in this pattern.

2 Press seams in one direction using starch to stabilize the panels as described on page 9 of the "Top Tips" chapter.

### CUT THE BLOCKS

3 Make several sets of freezer-paper templates A and B found on page 45. (Refer to page 9 of the "Top Tips" chapter for instructions on how to make and use freezer-paper templates.)

4 Adhere two sets of the A and B freezer-paper templates to a pieced panel *(Diagram 1)*.

5 Place the edge of a rotary-cutting ruler along a straight outer edge of the freezer-paper template and cut. Repeat for all straight edges. Cut the curved edges with scissors.

6 From the pieced panels, cut a total of 54 A's and 54 B's.

7 Sort the pieces into contrasting AB pairs (i.e., light A's with dark B's, dark A's with a light B's).

8 Stitch the pairs together to make Drunkard's Path blocks. Make 54 *(Diagram 2)*.

*Diagram 2* **Drunkard's Path Blocks**

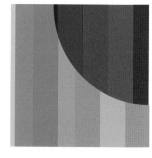

9 From the remaining medium to dark scraps, stitch a 22" x 3½ yard panel. Cut twenty-six 9½" squares from the panel. These are border squares *(Diagram 3)*.

*Diagram 3*
**Border Square**

# Quilt Assembly

1 On the design wall, lay out 48 Drunkard's Path blocks in 8 rows of 6. Refer to the quilt photo (page 40) and Quilt Assembly Diagram (below) for placement ideas, or create your own placement pattern. (See diagrams on page 44 for pattern variations.)

2 Stitch the blocks into rows and join the rows, carefully matching seams.

3 Lay out 4 border blocks and 4 of the remaining Drunkard's Path blocks in a row. Alternate the direction of the strips in the squares vertically and horizontally, as shown. Stitch them into a side border of 8 blocks. Make a second side border using the remaining Drunkard's Path blocks and 6 border blocks.

4 Stitch the side borders to the long sides of the quilt.

5 Lay out 8 border blocks, alternating vertical and horizontal placement as before, and stitch them together to make a border. Make 2. Stitch the borders to the top and bottom of the quilt.

6 Quilt as desired. Bind the quilt using the 2" × 44" dark print strips, following the binding instructions on page 17 in the "Top Tips" chapter.

**Note:** *You may certainly take artistic license with your quilt and use as many or as few of the remaining 6 Drunkard's Path blocks as you'd like.*

*Quilt Assembly Diagram*

side border

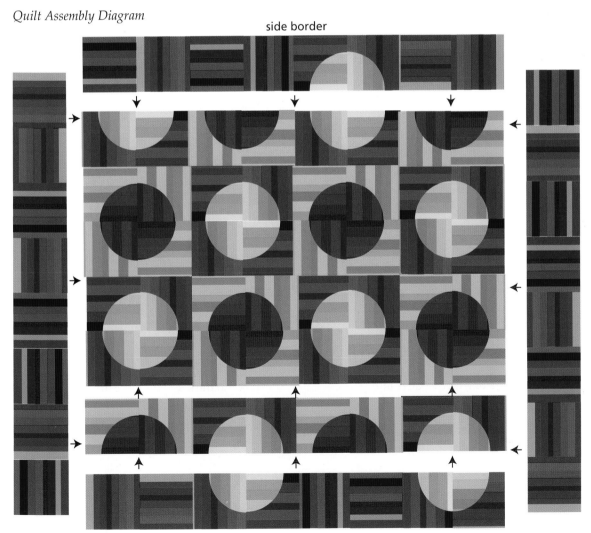

side border

*Variation 1*

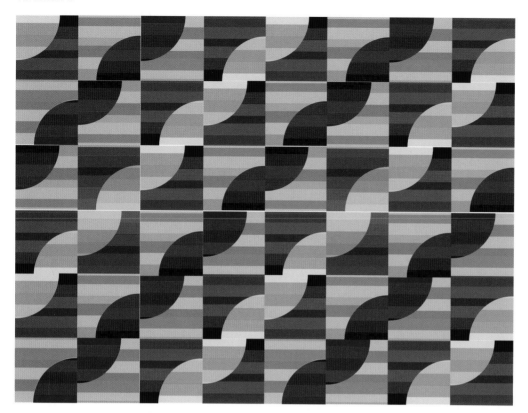

There are many creative ways to assemble the 48 Drunkard's Path blocks. These variations are just a few of the possibilities.

You also may vary the border blocks or maintain the alternating vertical and horizontal placement to complete the border and finish the quilt variation you design.

*Variation 2*

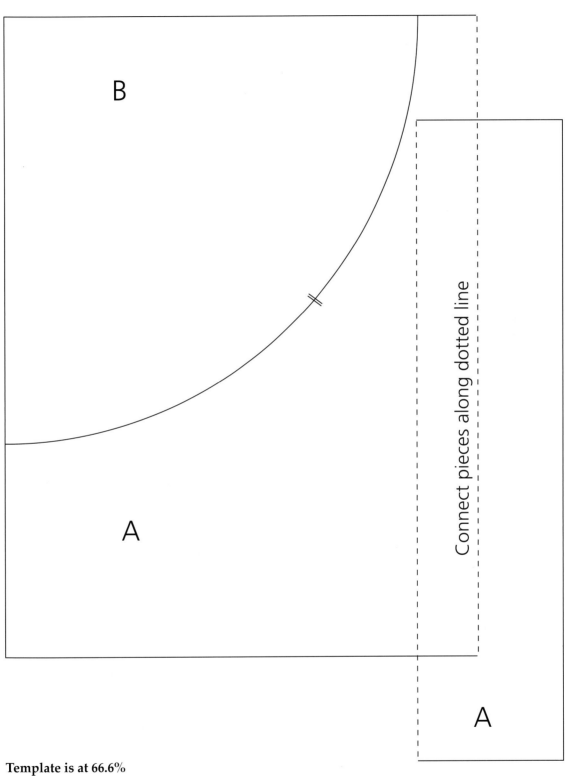

B

A

Connect pieces along dotted line

A

**Template is at 66.6%**
**Enlarge on photocopier at 150%**

# Plaid Poppies

Finished dimensions: 51½" × 64"

Finished background block: 7½" × 10"

Difficulty: Intermediate

## Materials

- White, off-white, ecru, beige, and tan print scraps or Fat Quarters (18" × 22") to equal 2 yards

- Pink, red, orange, and violet plaid and print scraps to equal ¾ yard, for the poppies

- Green, blue, gray, and brown plaid and print scraps to equal 1 yard, for the leaves and poppy stems

- 2½ yards of dark red plaid, for the inner and outer borders and binding

- ¾ yard of white and red plaid, for the middle border

- 5 yards of backing fabric

- Twin-size batting

- 2 yards of paper-backed fusible web (My favorite brand is Trans-Web. See Resources on page 79 for more information.)

The leftover pieces from Dad's Plaids reminded me of the colors of oriental poppies. Long stems with mounds of leaves at the base create a graceful arrangement on my quilt. My great-aunt Selma Reusser lived next door to my family when I was growing up. She was a prolific gardener and took the time to teach me all the names of the flowers in her yard. I was most fascinated with her poppies and how they would magically pop open at sunrise. I now grow them in my own flower gardens and think of her when the poppies bloom. But I also have poppies blooming on my wall year-round to remind me of her patience and love.

the width of the rectangle (horizontal rectangle). (*Diagram 1*).

*Diagram 1*

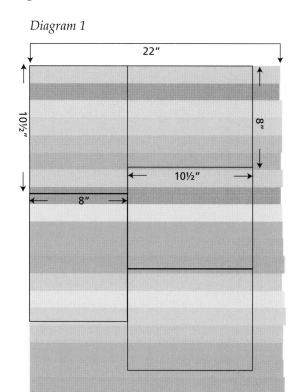

# Cutting

### FOR THE BACKGROUND AND BORDERS

1 Cut the white, off-white, ecru, beige, and tan prints into 1½"- to 3"-wide × 22"-long strips.

2 Cut 8: 1" × 44" strips of green, blue, gray, and brown plaid or print strips, for the poppy stems.

3 Cut 2: 1¼" × 50½" lengthwise strips of dark red plaid, for the inner border.

4 Cut 2: 1¼" × 39½" lengthwise strips of dark red plaid, for the inner border.

5 Cut 4: 6" × 55" lengthwise strips of dark red plaid, for the outer border.

6 Cut 4: 2" × 60" lengthwise strips of dark red plaid, for the binding.

7 Cut 6: 1" × 38" bias strips of red and white plaid, for the middle border.

# Directions

### FOR THE QUILT BACKGROUND

1 Stitch the white, off-white, ecru, beige, and tan print strips together along their length to make a panel at least 22" wide and 3½ yards long. Press the seams in one direction.

2 Cut twenty-five 8" × 10½" rectangles from the panel. Thirteen should have the strips running the length of the rectangle (vertical rectangle), and twelve should have the strips running across

3 Lay out the blocks in 5 rows of 5, alternating the vertical and horizontal rectangles. I suggest placing the darker blocks in the lower portion of the quilt center and the lighter blocks in the upper portion of the quilt center.

4 Stitch the blocks into rows and join the rows (*Diagram 2*).

### FOR THE APPLIQUÉS

5 Cut the pink, red, orange, and violet plaids and prints into 1½"-wide to 3"-wide strips and stitch them together along their length. I suggest varying from light to dark and from color to color along the length of your panel. Make a panel at least 22" × 1 yard in length, or use panel pieces left over from Dad's Plaids. Press the seams in one direction.

6 Trace poppy shapes from the line drawing provided on page 51 on the paper side of the fusible webbing. Note that each poppy on the drawing is slightly different. Note, too, that the poppies are

*Diagram 2*

made of varying numbers of pieces (from 4 to 8). Use the photograph on page 46 and the line drawing on page 51 for inspiration.

Make enough shapes for 8 complete poppies. I suggest making 3 large poppies and 5 small poppies, or draw your own original flower shapes and buds on the paper side of the paper-backed fusible web. Loosely cut out the shapes, leaving a ¼" margin outside the drawn lines.

7  Fuse the shapes to the wrong side of the pink, red, orange, and violet plaid and print panel according to the manufacturer's instructions. Cut the shapes out exactly on the drawn lines.

8  Remove the paper backing and arrange the shapes for one poppy to make a flower on a Teflon

**Note:** *For exact placement and appliqués shaped identically to mine, you may enlarge the line drawing on page 51 by 600% at your copy shop and use it for your appliqué templates and placement pattern.*

press sheet. Fuse. Cool. Remove the poppy from the Teflon press sheet. Repeat this process for each poppy. Set them aside.

9  Cut the blue, green, gray, and brown plaids and prints into 1½"-wide to 3"-wide strips and stitch them together along their length. Make a panel at least 22" × 1 yard in length, or use panel pieces left over from Dad's Plaids. I suggest moving from dark values to light values along the length of this panel. Press the seams in one direction.

10  Enlarge and trace the leaf shapes from the 4 pieces provided on page 50 on the paper side of the fusible webbing to make at least 12 large leaves and 15 small leaves. Loosely cut out the shapes, leaving a ¼" margin outside the drawn lines.

11  Fuse the shapes to the wrong side of the blue, green, gray, and brown plaid and print panel according to the manufacturer's instructions. Cut the shapes out exactly on the drawn lines. I suggest making both large and small leaves in both light and dark values. Remove the paper backing. Set them aside while preparing the quilt background and borders.

# Quilt Assembly

1  Press both of the long edges of the 1" × 44" blue, green, gray, and brown plaid or print strips under ¼". Set them aside.

2  Using a ruler, draw straight lines on the quilt background to indicate where the eight poppy stems will go. Refer to the line drawing on page 51 for placement ideas.

3  Appliqué the prepared blue, green, gray, and brown plaid or print strips along the marked lines to make the poppy stems.

4  Stitch the 1¼" × 50½" dark red plaid strips to the long sides of the quilt center. Press the seams toward the dark red plaid.

5 Stitch the 1¼" × 39½" dark red plaid strips to the top and bottom of the quilt center. Press, as before. Press all seams in the subsequent borders in the same manner.

6 Stitch the 1" × 38" red and white plaid bias strips together, end-to-end, to make a long middle border.

7 Measure the length of the quilt center including the borders. Cut 2 lengths of the red and white plaid middle border to that measurement and stitch them to the sides of the quilt.

8 Measure the width of the quilt, including the borders. Cut 2 lengths of the middle border to that measurement and stitch them to the top and bottom of the quilt.

9 In the same manner, measure, trim, and stitch two of the 6" × 55" dark red plaid strips to the sides of the quilt. Measure, trim, and stitch the remaining 6" × 55" dark red plaid strips to the top and bottom of the quilt.

10 Position the prepared poppies in place at the top of the poppy stems. Fuse according to the manufacturer's instructions for the fusible webbing product.

11 Position the darkest leaves in place along the lower portion of the quilt at the base of the poppy stems. Use your own judgment for placement or refer to the line drawing on page 51 and the quilt photo on page 46 for ideas. Some lower leaves should overlap the bottom border. Fuse in place.

12 Position the lighter leaves on top of or near the dark leaves. The dark leaves will appear to recede into the background, and the light leaves will come forward visually to make the foreground. Refer to the line drawing on page 51 and the quilt photo on page 46 as needed. Fuse in place.

13 Finish the appliqué edges, using your choice of satin stitch, blanket stitch, or free-motion straight stitch.

14 Quilt as desired. Bind the quilt using the 2" × 60" dark red plaid strips, following the binding instructions on page 17 in the "Top Tips" chapter.

**Templates are at 33%**
**Enlarge on photocopier at 300%**

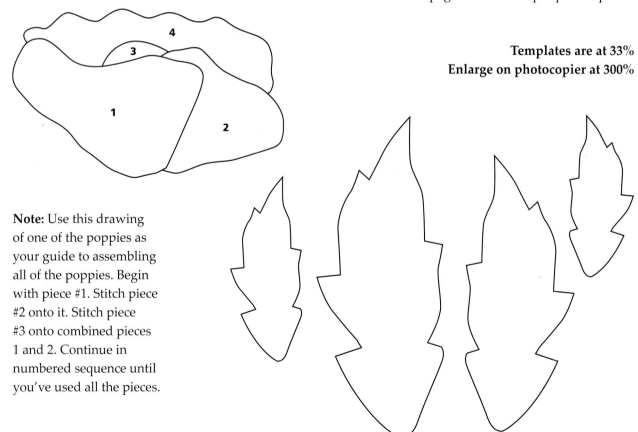

**Note:** Use this drawing of one of the poppies as your guide to assembling all of the poppies. Begin with piece #1. Stitch piece #2 onto it. Stitch piece #3 onto combined pieces 1 and 2. Continue in numbered sequence until you've used all the pieces.

**Template is at 16.67%**
**Enlarge on photocopier at 600%**

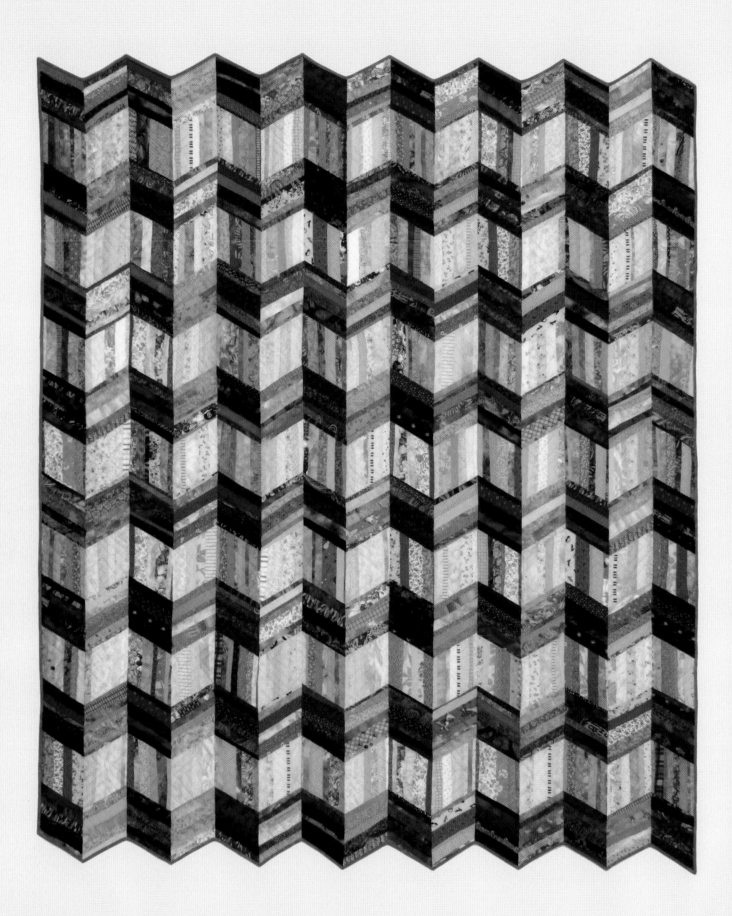

52

# Picket Fence

Finished dimensions: 82½" × 91½"
Finished block size: 5½" 60° diamonds
Difficulty: Intermediate

## Materials

- Assorted dark print scraps to equal at least 3½ yards
- Assorted medium print scraps to equal at least 5½ yards
- Assorted light print scraps to equal at least 3 yards
- 1¼ yards of medium blue print, for the binding
- 6 yards of backing fabric
- Queen-sized batting

Value plays an important role in creating the illusion of depth and layers in this quilt. Careful placement of lights, mediums, and darks is not required but will really enhance the 3–D effect. This is truly a "stash–buster" quilt. There are no borders, so you don't need to buy new fabric. The quilt is stitched entirely from strips of scrap fabrics. Of course, if you wish, you can purchase new fabrics to make your version. (*This quilt was machine-pieced by Janice Unruh and long-arm machine-quilted by Shirley Gingerich.*)

# Cutting

1 Cut 1½"- to 3"-wide strips, print scraps. Sort them by value into light, medium, and dark groups.

2 Cut 7: 2" × 60" bias strips medium blue print, for the binding.

# Directions

### STITCH THE FABRICATED YARDAGE

1 Stitch the dark print strips together along their length to make a panel approximately 44" wide and at least 2½ yards in length. If you are using 22" long strips, make 2 panels at least 2½ yards long. Press the seams in one direction, using starch to stabilize the panels as described on page 9 in the "Top Tips" chapter.

2 In a similar manner, make two medium print panels 2½ yards long. If using 22" strips, make 4 panels. Press.

3 Make a light print panel 2½ yards long, as before. If using 22" strips, make 2 panels. Press.

### CUT THE BLOCKS

4 Lay out a dark print panel and cut a 6"-wide strip across one end. Lay the 60° line of a 6"-wide rotary-cutting ruler on a cut edge of the strip, and make the first cut. Measure and cut 6" away from and parallel

to the first cut, to make a 60° diamond. Cut a total of 64 dark diamonds (*Diagram 1*).

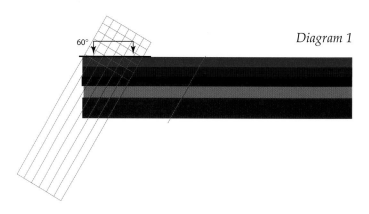

*Diagram 1*

5 Lay out a light print panel and cut diamonds as for the dark print diamonds. Cut a total of 49 light diamonds.

6 Lay out a medium print panel, and cut diamonds in the opposite direction as the dark and light panels. Cut a total of 112 medium diamonds (*Diagram 2*).

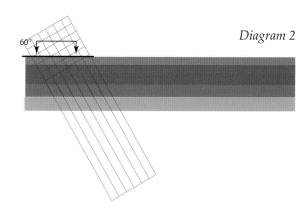

*Diagram 2*

7 You should have cut a total of 225 diamonds. The strips should run in the same direction for the light and dark diamonds, and in the opposite direction for the medium diamonds (*Diagram 3*).

*Diagram 3*

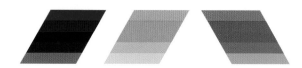

# Quilt Assembly

1 On the design wall, lay out the diamonds in 15 horizontal rows of 15 each, according to this pattern: For odd-numbered rows: Strips in the diamonds positioned horizontally; dark/medium/dark/medium, etc. For even numbered rows: Strips in the diamonds positioned vertically; medium/light/medium/light, etc. Refer to the quilt photo on page 52 and the Quilt Assembly Diagram on this page.

2 Stitch the blocks into *vertical* rows. Press seams of vertical rows A, C, E, G, and so on toward the top.

Press seams of the alternating vertical rows (B, D, F, and so on) toward the bottom.

3 Join the rows, carefully matching seams. Press these seams in one direction.

4 Quilt as desired. Bind the quilt using the 2" × 60" medium blue print bias strips, following the binding instructions on page 17 in the "Top Tips" chapter. Refer to the mitered corner instructions and Diagrams 13–15 (also on page 17) to complete the zigzag edges on the top and bottom of the quilt.

*Quilt Assembly Diagram*

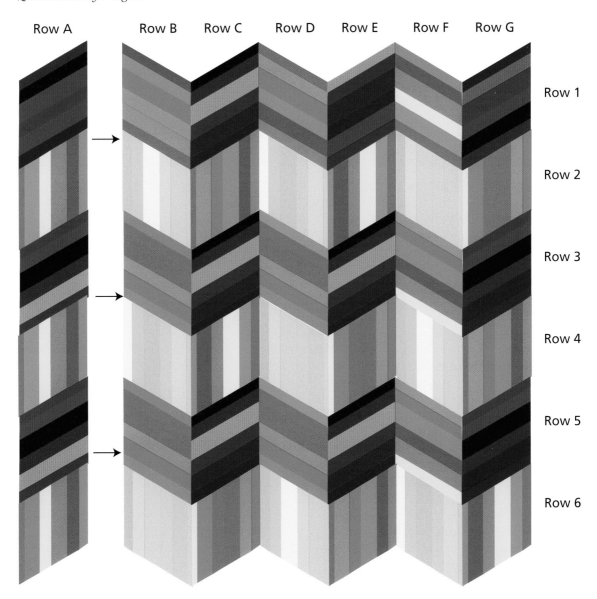

55

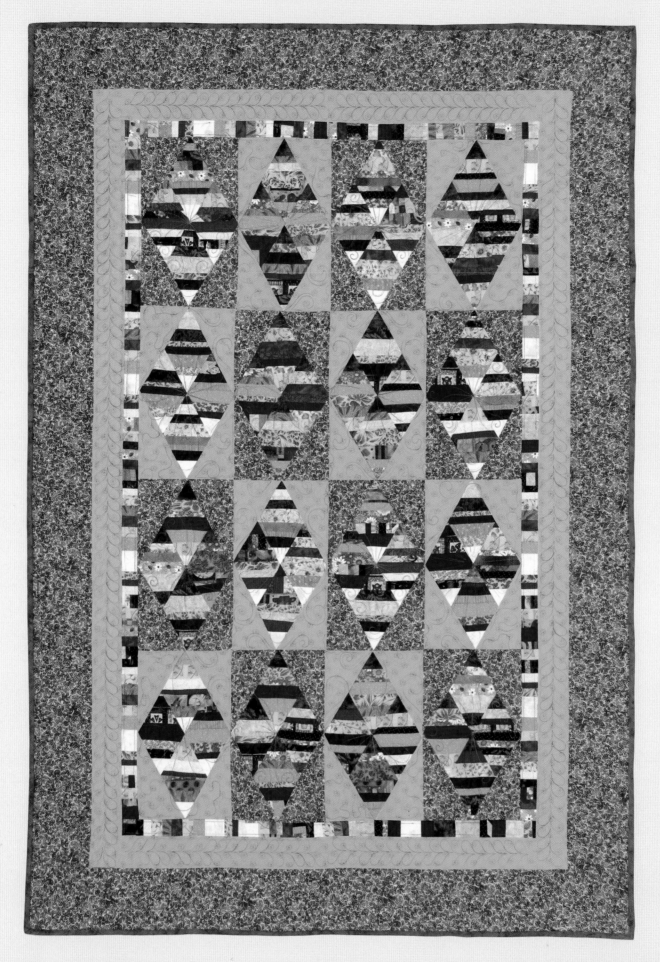

# Diamond in the Rough

Finished dimensions: 58" × 84"

Finished block size: 4" 60° triangles

Difficulty: Intermediate

## Materials

- 16 Fat Quarters of assorted prints, or equivalent in scraps, to a total of 4 yards
- 2 yards of green print, for the corner triangles and middle border
- 2½ yards of teal print, for the corner triangles and outer border
- ¾ yard of turquoise solid, for the binding
- 5¼ yards of backing fabric
- Full-sized batting

Mary Nielsen arrived at my string–quilt workshop with a bag of mismatched strips of fabric and her sewing machine. As is usual with makers of string-pieced quilts, she had an idea in mind when she began cutting triangles from her pieced panel, but changed her mind along the way after sewing six of them together into a hexagon. Mary said, "After stitching six small triangles together I realized three things: 1) The triangles were too small, 2) I would have to draft some odd–shaped pieces to set the resulting hexagons together, and 3) The pieced block looked amazingly like a Hazmat symbol."

She decided to stitch the triangles into diamonds, and stitched those diamonds in sets of four to make larger diamonds. Then she drafted the green and teal setting triangles, and the appealing result of all her hard work is evident. (*This quilt was machine-pieced and machine-quilted by Mary Nielsen.*)

# Cutting

1 Cut 1½"-wide to 3"-wide × 22"-long strips, assorted prints.

2 Cut 16 each: A and B (see page 61) from the green print.

3 Cut 16 each: A and B (see page 61) from the teal print.

4 Cut 2: 3½" × 70" green print strips, for the middle border.

5 Cut 2: 3½" × 50" green print strips, for the middle border.

6 Cut 2: 6½" × 75" teal print strips, for the outer border.

7 Cut 2: 6½" × 62" teal print strips, for the outer border.

8 Cut 8: 2" × 44" strips turquoise solid, for the binding.

# Directions

### STITCH THE FABRICATED YARDAGE

1 Stitch the assorted print strips together along their length, in no particular pattern, to make a panel approximately 3 yards in length.

2 Press seams in one direction, using starch to stabilize the panels as described on page 9 in the "Top Tips" chapter.

### CUT THE DIAMONDS

3 Make 4 freezer-paper templates from the diamond pattern on page 61. (Refer to page 9 of the "Top Tips" chapter for instructions on how to make and use freezer-paper templates.)

4 Adhere the diamond templates on the pieced panel with the widest part across the stripes. Cut along the outer edges of the templates, using a rotary cutter and ruler *(Diagram 1)*.

*Diagram 1*

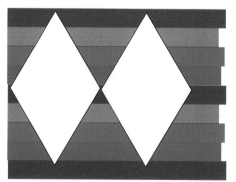

5 Remove the freezer-paper templates and adhere them on the panel, as before, and cut. *Remember to add a ¼" seam allowance to all sides of the template as you cut.* Make a total of 64 diamonds. Reserve the remaining portion of the panel for the inner border.

6 Lay out 4 diamonds in 2 diagonal rows of 2. Stitch the blocks into rows and join the rows to make a large diamond. Make 16 *(Diagram 2)*.

*Diagram 2*

7 Stitch 2 teal print corner triangles (A) and 2 teal print reversed corner triangles (B) to form a rectangle. Make 8 teal rectangle blocks *(Diagram 3)*.

*Diagram 3*

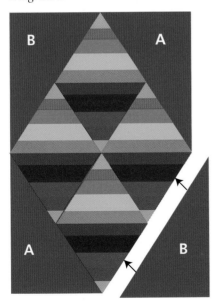

8 In the same manner, stitch green print corner triangles to the remaining large diamonds. Make 8 green rectangle blocks.

# Quilt Assembly

1 Lay out the rectangles in 4 rows of 4, alternating green and teal print rectangles.

2 Stitch the blocks into rows and join the rows.

3 Cut the remaining portion of the pieced panel into 2"-wide strips with the pieced strips running across the border (Diagram 4).

*Diagram 4*

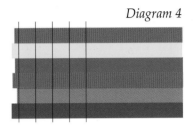

4 Measure the length of the quilt through the center. Stitch enough 2"-wide strips together end-to-end, to make an inner border that length, trimming as needed to fit. Make 2.

5 Stitch the inner borders to the sides of the quilt.

6 In the same manner, measure the width of the quilt through the center. Stitch 2"-wide strips together to make borders for the top and bottom of the quilt. Stitch them to the top and bottom of the quilt.

7 Measure the length of the quilt including the borders through the center. Trim the 3½" × 70" green print strips to that measurement and stitch them to the sides of the quilt.

8 Measure the width of the quilt including the borders. Trim the 3½" × 50" green print strips and stitch them to the top and bottom of the quilt.

9 In the same manner, measure, trim, and stitch the 6½" teal print outer borders to the quilt.

10 Quilt as desired. Bind the quilt using the 2" × 44" turquoise solid strips, following the binding instructions on page 17 in the "Top Tips" chapter.

*Quilt Assembly Diagram*

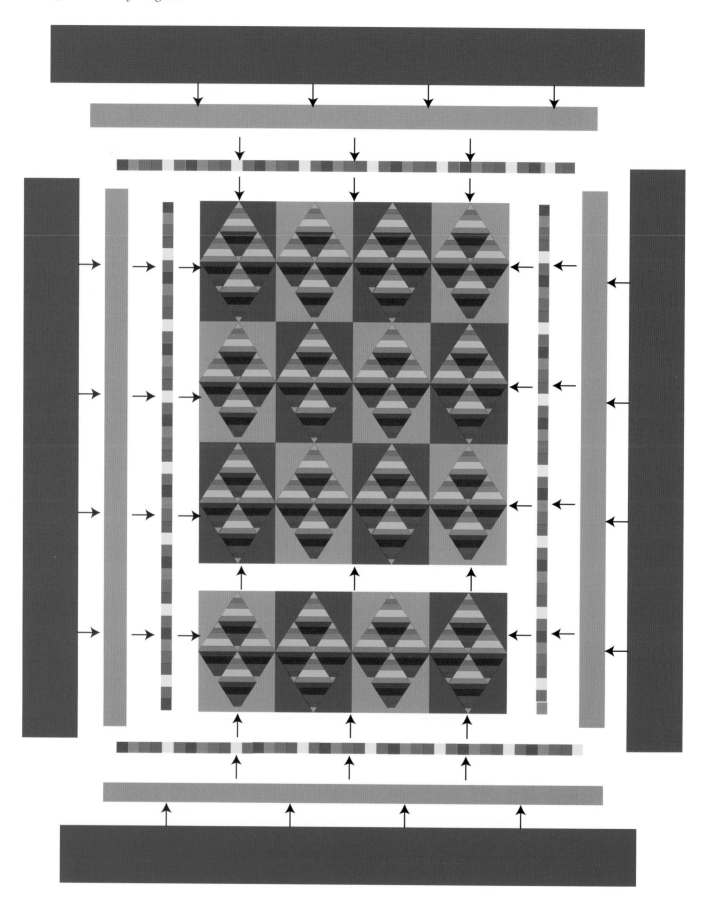

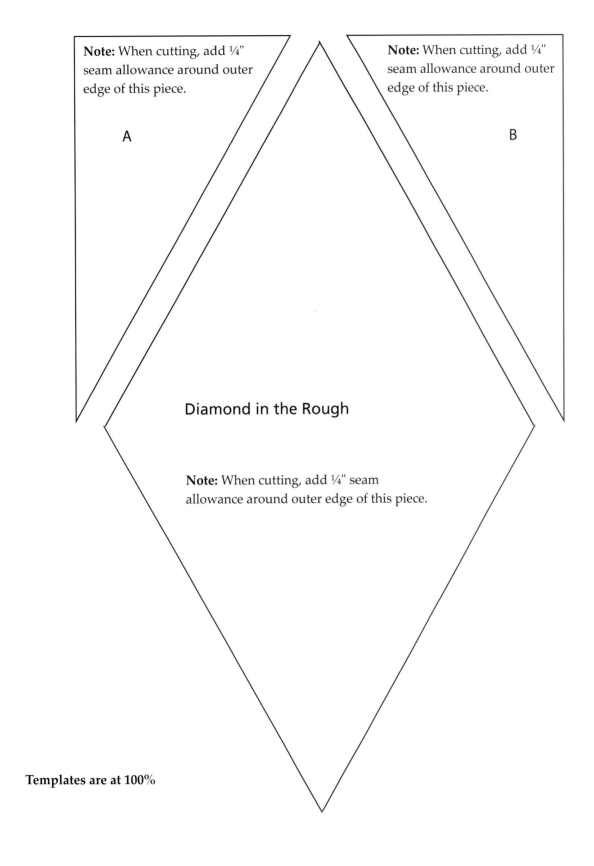

**Note:** When cutting, add ¼"
seam allowance around outer
edge of this piece.

A

**Note:** When cutting, add ¼"
seam allowance around outer
edge of this piece.

B

Diamond in the Rough

**Note:** When cutting, add ¼" seam
allowance around outer edge of this piece.

**Templates are at 100%**

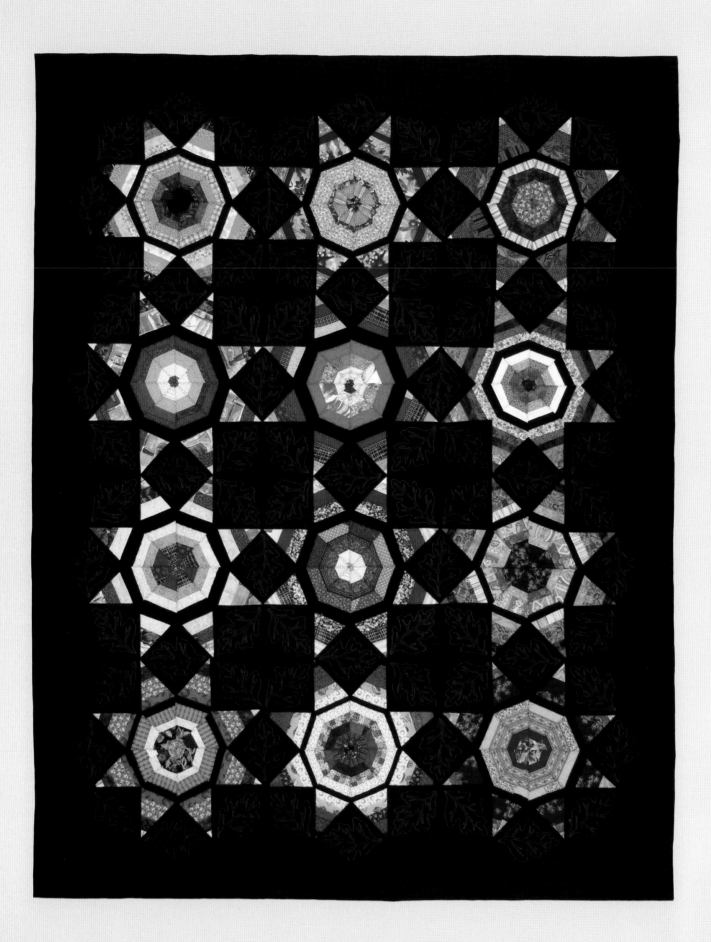

# Autumn Stars

Finished dimensions:  72" × 92"

Finished star block size:  20" square

Difficulty:  Experienced (Y-seams)

## Materials

- Assortment of print scraps to total 6 yards
- 6½ yards of black solid
- 5½ yards of backing fabric
- Queen-sized batting

Juxtaposing the multiple colors and prints of string stars with a black background creates a striking and graphic quilt. After planting 40 little oak trees on our property last fall, I decided that pumpkin-colored oak leaves would make an appropriate quilting pattern for this quilt. The outline quilting design is included with this pattern, if you wish to use it. I traced the outline on template plastic and cut it out. Then I traced around it in each square and around the stars, rotating it to keep it in the same position on each square. A heavier 30-weight thread (YLI Jeans Stitch, see Resources on page 79 for more information) was used for the machine quilting so that the leaf pattern would be visible on the black background.

# Cutting

1 Cut 1"-wide to 3"-wide × 44"-long strips from the print scraps.

2 Cut 24: 1½" to 3"-wide × 44" strips from the black solid.

3 Cut 48: 7½" squares from the black solid.

4 Cut 12: 12" squares from the black solid, then cut the squares in quarters diagonally to make 48 setting triangles.

5 Cut 2: 6½" × 82" lengthwise strips from the black solid, for the border.

6 Cut 2: 6½" × 75" lengthwise strips from the black solid, for the border.

7 Cut 9: 2½" × 44" strips from the black solid, for the binding.

# Directions

## STITCH THE FABRICATED YARDAGE

1 Stitch the scrap print strips together along their length, adding a black solid strip in the sequence approximately every 6 to 7 inches. Make 2 panels, each approximately 44" × 2½ yards in length.

2 Press seams in one direction, using starch to stabilize the panels as described on page 9 of the "Top Tips" chapter.

## CUT THE DIAMONDS

3 Make 8 freezer-paper templates from the template pattern provided on page 67. (Refer to page 9 in the "Top Tips" chapter for instructions on how to make and use freezer-paper templates.) Adhere the freezer-paper templates on a panel with the widest part of the diamond on or very near a black strip. All 8 templates should be positioned on or near the same black strip along the panel *(Diagram 1)*.

*Diagram 1*

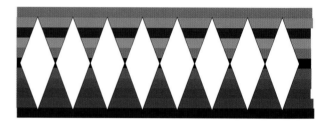

4 Using a rotary cutter and ruler, carefully cut the diamonds out of the panel.

5 Remove the freezer-paper templates. Adhere them to the panel, as before, with the widest part on or very near the next black strip, and cut a second set of diamonds. Cut a total of 12 sets of 8 diamonds. *Remember to add a ¼" seam allowance to all sides of the template as you cut.*

# Stitch the Stars

1 Lay out 8 matching diamonds, 4 black solid corner squares and 4 black solid setting triangles.

2 Place a 7½" black solid square on a diamond right sides together and stitch, starting and back-stitching ¼" from the inner edge to make a corner unit *(Diagram 2)*. Press the seam toward the square *(Diagram 3)*. Make 4. Set them aside.

*Note: The black solid squares and triangles are oversized to allow for trimming later.*

*Diagram 2*

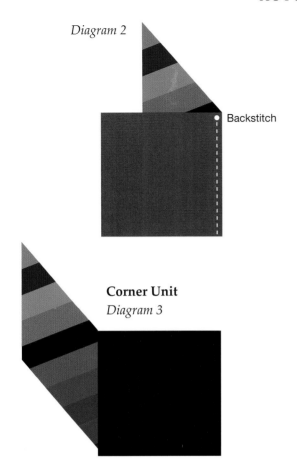

Backstitch

**Corner Unit**
*Diagram 3*

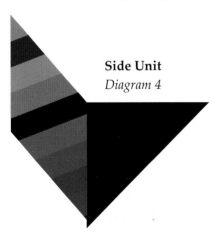

3 In the same manner, stitch a black solid setting triangle to a diamond, to make a side unit. Press the seam toward the triangle *(Diagram 4)*. Make 4.

**Side Unit**
*Diagram 4*

4 Lay a side unit on a corner unit, right sides together, aligning the star points. Stitch, starting and backstitching exactly at the end of the previous seam *(Diagram 5)*.

*Diagram 5*

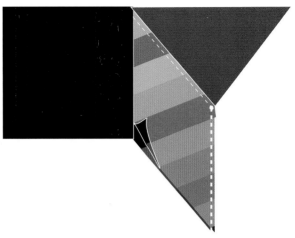

5 Refold the unit to stitch the triangle to the opposite star point, to make a quarter-star unit *(Diagram 6)*. Make 4.

*Diagram 6*     **Quarter-Star Unit**

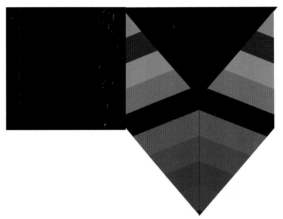

6 In a similar manner, join 2 quarter-star units to make a half-star unit *(Diagram 7)*. Make 2.

*Diagram 7*     **Half-Star Unit**

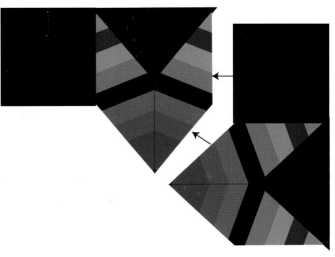

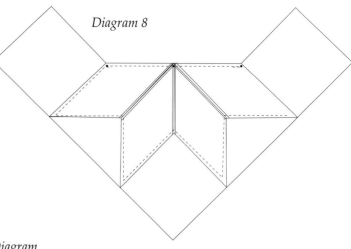

*Diagram 8*

7 Lay half-star units right sides together, matching the centers. Stitch, starting, stopping, and backstitching ¼" from each end *(Diagram 8)*.

8 Stitch the remaining triangles and squares to the star points to make the string star block. Press the seams toward the triangles and squares. Make 12.

9 Trim the star blocks to 20½" square or ¼" outside the diamond points.

# Quilt Assembly

1 Lay out the star blocks in 4 rows of 3. Stitch the blocks into rows and join the rows.

2 Measure the length of the quilt through the center of the quilt. Trim the 6½" × 82" black solid strips to that measurement and stitch them to the sides of the quilt.

3 Measure the width of the quilt including the borders. Trim the 6½" × 75" black solid strips to that length and sew them to the top and bottom of the quilt.

4 Quilt as desired or use the oak leaf quilting pattern on page 67, if you choose. Bind the quilt using the 2" × 44" black solid strips, following the binding instructions on page 17 in the "Top Tips" chapter.

*Quilt Assembly Diagram*

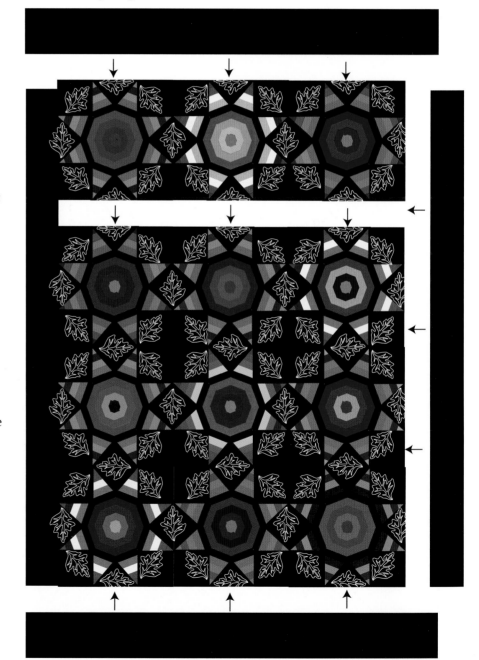

**Template is at 100%**

Black stripe across
widest part of diamond

*(Add ¼" seam allowances to
outer edges when cutting.)*

Oak Leaf Quilting Pattern

# Square Dance

Finished dimensions: 76½" × 93½"
Finished star block size: 6" and 8½" squares
Difficulty: Beginner

## Materials

- Assorted red, off-white to tan, and blue print scraps to equal 9 yards
- 2½ yards of off-white print, for the setting triangles
- ¾ yard of dark blue print, for the binding
- 6 yards of backing fabric
- Queen-sized batting

Several years ago, my quilt guild, "Miss Kitty's Quilters," made string quilts for our community project quilts. My small group worked with leftover blocks that just happened to be in two different sizes. We found that the smaller block would equal the measurement of the larger block if set on–point. Setting triangles brought the smaller blocks up to size, and arranging them around a center of larger blocks created an edging that exactly fit the top of a queen–sized bed. This attractive pattern was repeated in my friend Cricket Turley's favorite cowboy colors of reds, tans, and blues to make Square Dance. (*This quilt was machine-pieced by Cricket Turley and Elsie Campbell. Long-arm machine-quilted by Shirley Gingerich.*)

# Cutting

1 Cut various width strips from the red, off-white to tan, and blue print scraps. Strips should vary in width from approximately 2" to 3" and may be assorted lengths, but preferably at least 22" long.

2 Cut 12: 10¼" squares of off-white print, then cut them in quarters diagonally to make 48 setting triangles.

3 Cut 8: 6⅞" squares of off-white print, then cut them in half diagonally to make 16 corner triangles.

4 Cut 9: 2" × 44" strips from various prints, for the binding.

# Directions

### STITCH THE FABRICATED YARDAGE

1 Stitch the red, off-white to tan, and blue strips together along their length, in no particular pattern, to make a pieced panel. Use a variety of values and scales of prints. Make 6 panels approximately 22" × 2½ yards in length.

2 Press the seams in one direction. Use starch to stabilize the yardage, as described on page 9 of the "Top Tips" chapter.

### CUT THE BLOCKS

3 From the pieced panels, cut seventy-one 9" squares and twenty-eight 6½" squares. Set the 6½" squares and 36 of the 9" squares aside.

# Quilt Assembly

1 Lay out thirty-five 9" squares in 7 rows of 5, in a basket-weave pattern, as shown in the Quilt Assembly Diagram (on page 71). Stitch the squares into rows and join the rows. Set the quilt top aside.

2 Lay out a 6½" square and 2 setting triangles. Stitch the triangles to opposite sides of the 6½" square to make a border unit (Diagram 1). Make 10 side border units and 10 top and bottom border units.

*Diagram 1*

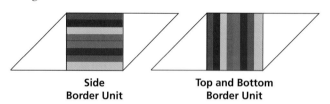

**Side
Border Unit**          **Top and Bottom
Border Unit**

3 Lay out a 6½" square, a setting triangle, and 2 corner triangles. Stitch the triangles to the 6½" square, to make a corner unit (Diagram 2). Make 4 side corner units and 4 top and bottom corner units.

*Diagram 2*

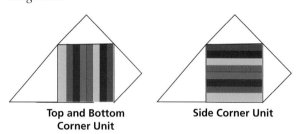

**Top and Bottom
Corner Unit**          **Side Corner Unit**

4 Stitch 5 side border units and 2 side corner units together to make a side pieced border (Diagram 3). Make 2.

*Diagram 3*

**Side Pieced Border**

**5** Stitch 5 top and bottom border units and 2 top and bottom corner units together to make a pieced top and bottom border. Make 2.

**6** Trim the outer edges of all borders ¼" outside the squares' corners.

**7** Stitch a trimmed side border to each long side of the quilt.

**8** Stitch a trimmed top and bottom border to the top and bottom of the quilt.

**9** Lay out nine 9" squares end-to-end, in basket-weave pattern, beginning and ending with a horizontal block. Stitch the squares together to make an outer border *(Diagram 4)*. Make 4.

*Quilt Assembly Diagram*

*Diagram 4*

**Outer Border**

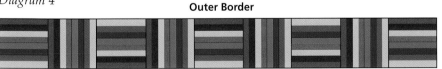

**10** Stitch an outer border to each long side of the quilt, matching the seams between blocks to the centers of the setting triangles' outer edges.

**11** In the same manner, stitch the remaining outer borders to the top and bottom of the quilt.

**12** Quilt as desired. Bind the quilt using the 2" × 44" dark blue print strips, following the binding instructions on page 17 in the "Top Tips" chapter.

# Gallery of
# String Quilts

## *Quilts that use long, vertical rows of strings*

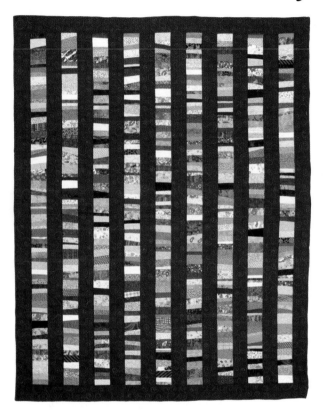

## Leftover Strings

**Starlyn Baker** of Ellicott City, Maryland, made Leftover Strings (63" × 88") from hundreds of 6"-long pieces of fabric. Green sashing between the long rows of scraps not only adds width to the quilt, but provides the contrast needed to emphasize the colorful strings. Variations in the widths of the string pieces add dynamic movement to the pattern. The simplicity of this design makes it easy for any quilter, new or experienced, to make. *(Machine-pieced by* **Starlyn Baker** *and machine-quilted by* **Cindy Wilson**.*)*

## Rose Haiku

Although it doesn't look anything like Starlyn Baker's Leftover Strings quilt, **Barbara Halbgewachs** of Dodge City, Kansas, used a similar technique to make Rose Haiku (25" × 26"). She stitched black and white print strips together to make a pieced panel, and then sliced the panel into vertical strips. She added black sashing between the strips and offset the print strips slightly, bargello style. One wider sashing strip features large, machine-embroidered pink roses. The asymmetrical design has a definite Asian feel. *(Machine-pieced, machine-embroidered, and machine-quilted by* **Barbara Halbgewachs**.*)*

# Quilts made from diagonally-cut squares

## Squares

**Louise Feldt** is a prolific maker of quilts for others and a member of Miss Kitty's Quilters of Dodge City, Kansas. She makes quilts for the club's community projects, donating quilts for victims who have lost their homes to fire, flood, or tornado. Her family members all benefit from her skills, too. Squares (48" × 57") was made as a result of my short lesson about string quilting at one club meeting. Louise says, "Making this quilt was a great way to use up all the scraps in colors I don't really like." Maybe she didn't like the colors, but I absolutely love the teals and greens in this quilt. *(Machine-pieced and machine-quilted by **Louise Feldt**.)*

# Quilts made from straight-cut squares

## Gradient Squares

If you look closely, you'll see a very large flower on a green background of strings in Gradient Squares (52" × 52"). If you look even closer, there are two embroidered butterflies in the very center. **Deborah Ross** of Tulsa, Oklahoma, carefully gradated the clear, bright colors in a virtual rainbow across her stunning wall quilt. This quilt was juried into the American Quilter's Society's Des Moines, Iowa, quilt show. *(Machine-pieced and machine-quilted by **Deborah Ross**.)*

# Quilts made from straight-cut squares

## Early Morning Breeze

Using leftover fabric strips from other quilts and jackets, **Anita Marsh** of Oswego, Illinois, first chose a wide range of colors for her workshop samples, ranging from deep purples and blues to hot reds and oranges. When she played with the blocks on the design wall, she realized that she actually had the makings of two separate quilts. Carefully arranging the blocks from light in the center to darks in the outermost parts, Anita made Early Morning Breeze (56" × 61") first. She says, "The quilt reminded me of an early morning clearing in the forest, so I added a few leaves. Some of the leaves are cut from the leftover string-pieced panel; others are just scraps from my sewing room." (*Machine-pieced and machine-quilted by **Anita Marsh**.*)

## Chinkapin and Red Oak Fall

Chinkapin and Red Oak Fall (76" × 92") is a sister quilt to Early Morning Breeze. After realizing that she could make two quilts from the blocks made during my string-pieced quilt workshop, **Anita Marsh** of Oswego, Illinois, separated her blocks into cool and warm colors. Anita says, "You can tell that red and yellow are my favorite colors, since this quilt is a lot larger than the first quilt." The leaves on the quilt are life-sized, the templates made from actual leaves she collected on a photo expedition with her husband. The name of the quilt comes from the kind of trees from which the leaves came. I particularly like the organically-shaped outer border. Anita really likes the freedom that string-piecing allows and encourages. (*Machine-pieced and machine-quilted by **Anita Marsh**.*)

# Quilts made from straight-cut squares

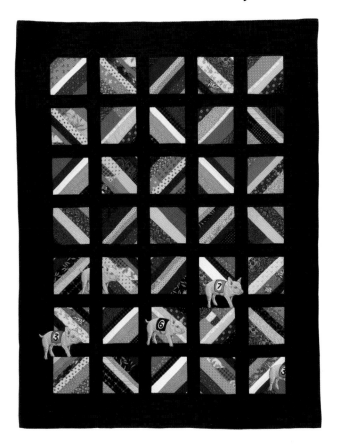

## Pigs in a Blanket

At first glance, Pigs in a Blanket (48" × 61") appears to be very traditional, but a second look reveals its whimsical nature. I collected fabrics with pigs for a few months because I wanted to make a quilt with this title. The racing pig print was the only pig fabric to appear in this quilt, but I had such fun deciding how to use it. I only had one Fat Quarter of this print and used nearly all the whole pigs in the print. (That's why there are a couple of pigs in parts on the quilt.) Light diagonals and black sashing give this quilt the appearance of having multiple layers. (*Machine-pieced, hand-appliquéd, and hand-quilted by* **Elsie M. Campbell**.)

# Quilts made from 45° triangles and diamonds

## String of Hearts

**Geri Pagliaro** of Wading River, New Jersey, says that making String of Hearts (58" × 70") was a fun way to take advantage of the red and white scraps of fabric in her collection. This quilt was begun in my String-Pieced Quilts workshop. Geri started with large white-on-white squares and red string-pieced squares cut on the bias. She drew a diagonal line through each white square, placed each white square right sides together with each red string-pieced square, and stitched through the squares ¼" on both sides of the line. Then, she cut the blocks apart on the marked line, to make 2 blocks. Playing on the design wall, she created her own unique setting for her blocks. (*Machine pieced by* **Geri Pagliaro** *and long-arm machine quilted by* **Anne Flynn**.)

# Quilts made from 45° triangles and diamonds

## Scrappy I

**Deborah Ross** of Tulsa, Oklahoma, says her passions are quilting and fiber arts. She loves working scrappy, including a multitude of different fabrics in one quilt. Scrappy I (58" × 50") was inspired by an episode of Simply Quilts on HGTV, but Debbie used her own artistic intuition for colors and value placement. This quilt has been juried into several prestigious quilt shows and was a First Place winner at the Oklahoma City Winter Quilt Show, 2009. *(Machine-pieced and machine-quilted by **Deborah Ross**.)*

## The Generation Quilt

**Susan Morgans Paul** and her daughters, **Megan Paul** and **Tracey Paul Houser**, participated in my String-Pieced Quilts workshop to make a single quilt. I enjoyed watching the cooperation and energy among mother and daughters as they worked together on this project. Because there were three working on one class project, the blocks were entirely finished before the daylong class ended. The Generation Quilt (58" × 84") involved more than two generations, however. The trio used fabrics donated by their grandmother and great-grandmother Sarah Lutz Keilman (101 years young) to make a quilt for the only non-quilting member of the multi-generational family, mother and grandmother, Elizabeth Keilman Morgans. *(Machine-pieced by **Sue Paul**, **Megan Paul**, and **Tracey Houser**; machine-quilted by **Barb Schoenauer**.)*

# Quilts that use other traditional patterns

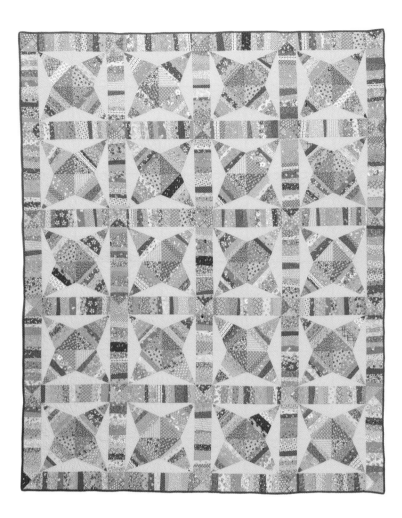

## Crossroads to Kansas

**Nancy Arseneault** of Tucson, Arizona, made Crossroads to Kansas (80" × 99") for her friend who lives in Kansas. Many traditional patterns can be enlarged so that pieces can be cut from string-pieced panels, as in this quilt. Nancy used additional strings for the pieced sashing and border. The predominant reds and yellows, with a sprinkling of green and blue, remind me of a bright spring day when the tulips and daffodils are in bloom. (*Machine-pieced by **Nancy Arseneault** and long-arm machine-quilted by **Barbara Angerhofer**.*)

## Ring Around the Roses

A love of pink that led to a huge collection of pink and black prints prompted **Barbara Halbgewachs** of Dodge City, Kansas, to make Ring Around the Roses (99" × 99") for her own bed. Barbara first cut very large squares from her string-pieced panels, not wanting to waste an inch of them. Then she drafted a large quarter-arc and made a template. She cut the squares into two pieces similar to the traditional Drunkard's Path block and added 1" black bias strips to make up for the fabric lost to seam allowances. The outcome is graphic, resulting in an ultra-modern-looking quilt. (*Machine-pieced and machine-quilted by **Barbara Halbgewachs**.*)

# Quilts that incorporate appliqué with strings

## Four Seasons Wreath

While I was growing up in the small Oklahoma town of Deer Creek, **Louise Krehbiel** was an integral part of that community. She was always a great supporter of my needlework skills through my 4-H and church activities. Louise made the appliqué pieces in my string-pieced appliqué class and was puzzled for a while as to what she could make from all the diverse colors. She didn't have to think very long before creating her Four Seasons Wreath (26" × 28"). Louise passed away in January 2008, but her daughter Beth Krehbiel Peters now proudly displays this quilt in her home. *(Machine-pieced and hand-quilted by Louise Krehbiel.)*

## String-Pieced Star

Several years ago, **Connie Olson** of Grand Island, Nebraska, enrolled in one of my string-piecing workshops with a particular quilt in mind. She'd seen a lovely Lone Star quilt patterned in a book, *Quick Quilts from the Heart* (Oxmoor House, 1994), by Marianne Fons and Liz Porter. In this pattern, the little star was surrounded by a series of borders and a little appliqué. After making the string-pieced star points in my class, Connie adapted the borders from the pattern and created her own version of String-Pieced Star (49" × 49"). *(Machine-pieced, hand-appliquéd, and hand-quilted by Connie Olson.)*

# Resources

## SEWING MACHINES

**Bernina models Artista 170, 200/730, and Aurora 430 sewing machines** were used to make the pattern quilts.

*Bernina of America, Inc.*
*3702 Prairie Lake Court*
*Aurora, IL 60504*
*www.berninausa.com*

## QUILTING THREAD

**YLI Jeans Stitch thread** was used for quilting Pots of Flowers border motifs and Autumn Stars oak leaf motifs.

*YLI Corporation*
*1439 Dave Lyle Blvd.*
*Rock Hill, SC 29730*
*www.ylicorp.com*

## FUSIBLE WEB

The paper-backed fusible webbing used to fuse the appliqués was **Lite Steam-a-Seam 2.**

*The Warm Company*
*5529 186th Place SW*
*Lynnwood, WA 98037*
*www.warmcompany.com*

## MARKING TOOLS

The **Bohin water-eraseable marking pen** was used to mark light-colored fabrics for quilting.

*Bohin France*
*St. Sulpice sur Risle*
*61300 L'Aigle FRANCE*
*www.bohin.fr/en/*

**The Nonce marking pencil by Collins®** was used to mark dark-colored fabrics for quilting.

*Distributed by*
*Prym Consumer USA Inc.*
*P.O. Box 5028*
*Spartanburg, SC 29304*
*www.dritz.com*

## PRESSING AIDS

**Teflon® Pressing Sheet** by June Tailor™ was used to fuse appliqué units.

*June Tailor™ Inc.*
*P.O. Box 208; 2861 Highway 175*
*Richfield, WI 53076*
*www.junetailor.com*

**Faultless Hot Iron Cleaner**™ is readily available at sewing and notion stores.

## LABELING PENS

**Sakura Pigma® pens** are archival-quality permanent ink pens that were used to make labels for the quilts.

*Sakura of America, Inc.*
*30780 San Clemente Street*
*Hayward, CA 94544*
*www.sakuraofamerica.com*

## OTHER TOOLS

**Susan Cleveland's Groovin' Piping Trimming Tool** was used to trim pipings to a consistent width for the oval frame on Pots of Flowers and for piped bindings on some quilts.

*Pieces Be With You*
*Susan K. Cleveland*
*54336 237th Ave.*
*West Concord, MN 55985*
*www.piecesbewithyou.com*

## BOOKS ABOUT COLOR AND DESIGN

*Color Mastery: 10 Principles for Creating Stunning Quilts* by Maria Peagler (Willow Ridge Press, 2008).

*Willow Ridge Press*
*10690 Big Canoe*
*Big Canoe, GA 30143-5133*
*www.colormastery.com*

*Color Play* by Joen Wolfrom (C & T Publishing, 2001).

*C&T Publishing, Inc.*
*1651 Challenge Drive*
*Concord, CA 94520-5206*
*www.ctpub.com*

# Acknowledgments

I'd like to thank:

- Merle and Phyllis Good for publishing this book.

- Delphine Martin for her expert editing skills and Jan Mast for her technical skills.

- Friends and workshop participants who contributed their time, expertise, and quilts for this book, in particular Mary Nielsen, Shirley Gingerich, Janice Unruh, Cricket Turley, and Cynthia Vierthaler.

- Delores Thompson and Dodge City High School for the use of the photo-graphy studio and Stephanie Willoughby Stewart for the cover photography.

- Chance and Mindy Morrow and Fergerson's Furniture and Appliance Store for on-location photography settings.

- Bernina for making the fine sewing machines on which the pattern quilts were stitched.

- My patient and kind husband, Ken Campbell, for pitching in with the household chores and cooking when I was too busy with this book.

# About the Author

Elsie Campbell is best known for her exquisite hand-quilted, award-winning quilts, but she started out, like many other quil-ters, in the field of dressmaking. She grew up in the small com-munity of Deer Creek, Oklahoma, attending the Deer Creek Men-nonite Church and learning her quilting skills from her mother and the Deer Creek Mennonite Women's Mission Society. After graduating from a small teachers col-lege in Oklahoma, she taught home econom-ics and special education in public schools.

Elsie began exhibiting her quilts nation-ally in 1992 and has won numerous presti-gious awards. Most recently, she won Best Machine Workmanship Awards at several national-level shows. Earlier awards include First Place in the traditional cat-egory at the International Quilt Festival in Houston, Texas; Best of Show at Quilt America! in Indian-apolis, Indiana; the Mary Krick-baum Award for Best Hand Quilting at the National Quilt Association Show; and the American Quilter's Society's Excellence in Hand Workmanship Purchase Award.

Elsie lives in Dodge City, Kansas, with her husband of 38 years, Kenneth. The couple has two grown sons.